Henry Brown

The Sonnets of Shakespeare Solved, and the Mistery of His Friendship,

Love, and Rivalry Revealed Illustrated by Numerous Extracts from the Poet's Work,

Contemporary Writers, and Others Authors

Henry Brown

The Sonnets of Shakespeare Solved, and the Mistery of His Friendship,
Love, and Rivalry Revealed Illustrated by Numerous Extracts from the Poet's Work,
Contemporary Writers, and Others Authors

ISBN/EAN: 9783337309909

Printed in Europe, USA, Canada, Australia, Japan

Cover: Foto ©Thomas Meinert / pixelio.de

More available books at **www.hansebooks.com**

THE

Sonnets of Shakespeare Solved,

AND THE

MYSTERY OF HIS FRIENDSHIP, LOVE, AND RIVALRY

REVEALED.

ILLUSTRATED BY NUMEROUS EXTRACTS FROM THE

POET'S WORKS, CONTEMPORARY WRITERS,

AND OTHER AUTHORS,

BY HENRY BROWN.

" Seal up the mouth of outrage for a while,
Till we can clear these ambiguities,
And know their spring, their head, their true descent."
Romeo and Juliet.

" Rare is true love, true friendship is still rarer."
La Fontaine.

LONDON:

JOHN RUSSELL SMITH,

36, SOHO SQUARE.

1870.

CONTENTS.

PREFACE.

The Sonnets of Shakespeare, till within the last few years, have been strangely neglected, and even now few readers of his dramatic works read these poems; they have been and still remain a sealed book to his world-wide admirers. Nothing at all satisfactory has appeared in elucidation of them, no key by which an admirer may discover the secrets they contain, and participate with "the poet of all time" in the mystic conceptions of his great mind, in the mystery of his love and friendship, in the self-recorded testimony of his hopes and fears, his joys and sorrows, in that which has glorified his brow or stamped vulgar scandal upon it. All this and more the Sonnets will reveal, if the reader will follow the poet through his involved meanings, and permit him to become as it were his own expositor—a privilege which Shakespeare has hitherto been denied. The Sonnets will then be found to add honour to his character as a man and his reputation as a poet. To effect this, the reader

B

is requested to bear in memory these lines from Pope's "Essay on Criticism," as especially essential in this instance :—

> " A perfect judge will read each work of wit
> With the same spirit that its author writ."

In reference to the theory now promulgated, I beg to inform my readers that it has been entertained for some years; and now, after long reflection and research, I am induced to publish my discoveries, hoping they may prove an advantage to all who may desire to understand the Sonnets of Shakespeare.

H. BROWN.

PRELIMINARY REMARKS.

THERE are many objections made to the Sonnets of Shakespeare, but they arise entirely from misunderstanding. Those who so misjudge should be told, as were the readers of the first folio of his dramatic works, to "read him therefore again and again, and if then you do not like him, surely you are in some manifest danger not to understand him."* If such a request was made for the Plays, how much more necessary is it for the Sonnets, which are throughout as dark as the Plays are clear!

The first question upon the subject is, Who was the friend spoken of so much in the poems in question? I answer, Master William Herbert, afterwards third Earl of Pembroke,† and him alone it is the object of these pages to establish as claiming the honour of the friendship of Shakespeare. It was to this nobleman and his brother, designated those "incomparable pair of brethren," that the first folio was dedicated, as the "remains of your servant Shakespeare," at the time when Lord Southamp-

---

* Preface to the edition of 1623.

† It is also to this nobleman's honour that to his patronage England can boast of one of her greatest architects, Inigo Jones.

ton, who was publicly known as our poet's earliest patron,
was living and in London. About the date this loving
friendship was contracted (1597), Lord Southampton
embarked as a volunteer in the expedition against Spain,
and in the following year he attended Essex to Ireland as
general of the horse, and subsequently, when Essex fell
under the royal displeasure, Southampton, who was
leagued with him in his mad-cap rebellion, was com-
mitted to the Tower, and although his life was spared, he
was kept in prison during the remainder of Elizabeth's
reign. (See Bell's Poems of Shakspeare, p. 36.) Our
poet himself, cautious against arousing the enmity of
church or state, would naturally turn to one cautious
and politic like himself, which Herbert was. Shakespeare
may also have offended the headstrong earl in seeking,
by good advice, to curb his wild career. This might
naturally lead to a transfer of friendship ; and the one
fact of Shakespeare not being known to pen consolatory
verses to Southampton when in prison for high treason,
as other poets were doing, significantly points to a
rupture between them. The reason of this is that Lord
Southampton was merely a patron sought for by the poet,
while Master Herbert proved more than patron, he
became Shakespeare's all unlooked-for constant friend,
from his youth upward. Hence the poet pays him a
higher compliment than Lord Southampton had received.
Master Herbert is the actual Adonis of the poem
addressed to him. I acknowledge that he is no new
claimant. My object is to add to the evidence already
brought forward in proof of his right to it, although
numerous critics assent to his being the man, among

whom is Mr. Hallam. But what is most to the purpose is that there is full agreement between that young lord and the youth described in the Sonnets. The beauty which distinguished him so much above others I am able to show, Shakespeare was not alone in extolling.

It may be asked why such addresses were penned to one of his own sex? The judicious Shakespeare could never have been guilty of such errors. If such an inquirer will turn to one of our poet's earliest Comedies —that humorous satire upon the fashionable jargon of the day, " Love's Labour's Lost"—he will there find that even in the dawn of genius he expressed a dislike to mistress adulation in such spruce affected terms, till in maturity he penned these diversions for the delight of his patron. These lines from the Comedy suffice to show the drift of the poet :—

"Tush! none but minstrels like of Sonnetting."

"Assist me, some extemporal god of rhyme, for I am sure I shall turn Sonnetteer."

"This is the liver vein, which makes flesh a deity ;
A green goose, a goddess: pure, pure idolatry.
God amend us, God amend! we are much out o' the way."

Thus in two important points Shakespeare differed from his contemporaries; he was averse to either making a green goose a goddess, i. e., mistress sonnetting, or to flatter every rhymester, to be, as was the custom, extolled in return.

I will now show the origin of the friendship between the patron and the poet, which the player editors affirm was prosecuted with so much favour. According to a letter written by Rowland White to Sir Robert Sidney, (brother to the author of the "Arcadia" dated April,

1597, and printed in the Sidney Papers, it was about this date that the accomplished youth obtained his father's sanction to live in London,* but it is highly probable he had visited the capital on several occasions before making it his abode. The earliest notice I find of his being in London is in the "Sidney Memoirs," Vol. 2. We there learn from one of White's letters, dated April 3, 1597, that he was then on a visit to the Sidneys:—"My Lord Herbert, coming into the garden ;" and probably it was the close connections he was making that induced him thus to solicit his father, as it must have been about this time that an acquaintanceship was formed between Shakespeare and this attractive young lord. It is described (Sonnet 25) as an "unlooked-for joy," intimating that the youth proffered his friendship to the poet. A supposition may be formed from some of the earliest Sonnets addressed to Master W. H. that the youth's mother, either directly or indirectly, instigated Shakespeare to advocate so strenuously for his young friend to contemplate at once yoking himself to the car of Hymen, though but seventeen years of age ; and by self-example the poet with a good grace might advocate such a course. This appears to be referred to in Sonnets 2 and 3, where the poet speaks of his children being his "old excuse" for his loss of youth, vigour, and appearance. Add to this the circumstance of the Countess of Pembroke being herself a poetess and patroness of poets, and it is but natural she would desire her "lovely boy"

---

* White says :—"My Lord Herbert hath with much ado brought his father to consent that he may live at London, yet not before the next spring." (*Letter to Sir R. Sidney,* April, 1597), but he was probably much engaged in London from the date, 1597.

to seek the companionship and guidance of such a poetic writer as the author of those majestic and delightful dramas which both herself and her husband had so often witnessed, and which had won for "gentle Shakespeare" "golden opinions from all sorts of people." This upon her part would be nothing uncommon, as it was then the custom to place noble youths with favourite poets. It is, however, unnecessary here to adduce the numerous instances which could be given to support this statement. That this was the case with Herbert there is some confirmation in the 77th Sonnet, in which the poet seeks to advance his friend's mental adornments: the youth's mother is also affectionately mentioned in the third Sonnet.

Support is given to the conjecture that it was at the desire of the Countess, that the invitations to marriage were penned from the circumstance of a plot having afterwards been formed, between the years 1599 and 1600, among the friends of the youth, to allure him into marriage with the niece of the Lord Admiral. They, however, overshot the mark. Rowland White, in recording this, says :—" My Lord Herbert is very well ; I don't find any disposition at all in this gallant young lord to marry." These events, according to the Rev. Joseph Hunter's opinion, incited Shakespeare to write the Comedy of "Much Ado about Nothing;" and from internal evidence, and Sonnet reference, which he did not adduce, the supposition will be found conclusively proved, and it will be also seen that both the Comedy and the Sonnets originated in Shakespeare's perceiving the distaste Herbert evinced towards marriage, probably

even before the youth's friends observed it, resolved to
show him what may be the result of his folly, to this
end produces those sprightly characters, Benedick and
Beatrice, who have the same distaste towards wedlock,
but become united at last; and as Herbert scorned a
mortal mistress, the poet weds him, much to the youth's
desire, to a divine one, his Muse. The result is, a poetical
memorial is begotten of the poet's youthful and beautiful
friend.

The earliest reference to be found to Shakespeare's
writing Sonnets is in Francis Meres' "Wit's Treasury"
of 1598. We are there told that "mellifluous, honey-
tongued Shakespeare" had produced "sugared Sonnets,"
which were then in circulation among his "private
friends." It was therefore probably in the spring of this
year that he commenced the Herbert series; and as
Meres was intimately acquainted with Shakspeare, as one
of the private friends, he may have been shown some of
the earliest of these honied verses. Meres foresaw that
they were but an overture to the concert which was to
follow, and in his account of the dramatic and poetic
labours of our poet, in the "Wit's Treasury," he concludes by announcing that some Sonnets of a private
nature were in progress; and as he gives Shakespeare a
full measure of praise, and in all available instances
extols the Pembroke family, he may have seen the
growing intimacy between our poet and his young
patron, and rejoiced at the event. Meres in 1602
became rector of Wing, in Rutlandshire, and continued
to hold it for the remainder of his life. He died there in
1646, in the eighty-first year of his age. At the date of

his publishing the above-mentioned volume he resided in Southwark, near the Globe Playhouse. He was held in high repute for his learning, and styles himself "Master of Artes of both Universities." Even had he written his discourse "Of our English Poets" previous to 1598, the reference to work Shakespeare had in hand could well have been inserted at that date. The following is the passage in his "Wit's Treasury" to which reference is now made :—" As the soul of Euphorbus was thought to live in Pythagoras, so the sweet witty soul of Ovid lives in mellifluous, honey-tongued Shakespeare : witness his Venus and Adonis, his Lucrece, his sugared Sonnets among his private friends."

Shakespeare, having commenced to write Sonnets, continued to pen them till about 1604, solely for his own and friends' gratification. The poet seems to have kept copies of them himself. The Sonnets appeared in print in 1609, which was the year in which he is supposed to have left his London residence for his permanent abode at Stratford. They are evidently in their proper order, and arranged into two divisions; their combined number is one hundred and fifty-four. The first portion, almost the bulk of the series, contains one hundred and twenty-six, and are evidently addressed to one person, the "patron friend." The concluding twenty-eight appear to be addressed to a mistress. It will be shown that both these and the poem to the friend are pre-eminently parodies.*

The title-page announces, in unusually large capitals,

---

* By a singular coincidence, the majestic classic parody upon Homer's heroes, "Troilus and Cressida," was also first published in that year, 1609.

the contents of the volume as " Shakes-peare's Sonnets
never before imprinted : At London by G. Eld for T. T.,
and are to be sold by William Apsley, 1609." On the
following leaf is inscribed the dedication, of which the
following is a copy :—

> TO. THE. ONLIE. BEGOETTER. OF.
> THESE. INSUING. SONNETS.
> M͏ͬ W. H. ALL. HAPPINESSE.
> AND. THAT. ETERNITIE.
> PROMISED.
> BY.
> OUR. EVER.-LIVING. POET.
> WISHETH.
> THE. WELL. WISHING.
> ADVENTURER. IN.
> SETTING.
> FORTH.
>   T. T.*

A fitting dedication this to the enigmatical contents of
the volume. From this it may be assumed that T. T.,
Thomas Thorpe,† the printer and publisher, received instructions from the poet himself, hence the result of this
singularity. For either Shakespeare or Herbert to appear
openly in the publication, would have been, from the
contents of the volume containing so much mutual glori-
fication, averse to the feelings of both the poet and patron.
Upon such a proceeding hear the poet express himself in
a passage from " Alls Well that Ends Well " :—

" Then we wound our modesty, and make foul the clearness of our deserv-
ings, when of ourselves we publish them."

---

* T. T.'s reason for placing his initials alone upon the title-page and
inscription appears to have been in humble imitation of W. H.

† That T. T. was Thomas Thorpe is proved by an entry on the Stationers'
Registers :—

"20 May, 1609.

"Tho. Thorpe]   a book called Shakespeare's Sonnets."

And again in " Troilus and Cressida " :—

> " The worthiness of praise distains his worth,
> If that the prais'd himself bring the praise forth."

This mutual praise being at once both parody and truth impelled the poet to take this course.

From the poems may be seen that they were intended for publication, and that too in the life-time of the friends : they also reveal that the poet was neither ashamed of their merit as the sweetest extraction of his muse, or of the motives which inspired him to pen them. After repeated perusals, I gather from various hints that Shakespeare could not openly publish the friendship to the world, on account of the disgrace his profession cast upon him, at which he unceasingly and bitterly laments. Had they not been bosom friends, he could have openly dedicated to Lord Herbert, as he has done to Southampton : but the burden of the song being upon their private friendship forbade it. It also prevented the poet from entering into any panegyrics upon the young lord's ancestors or parents, since he undoubtedly would gladly have extolled that bright star of their coronet, Sir Philip Sidney, and his ever memorable sister Mary, Countess of Pembroke (to whom the " Arcadia " was dedicated as the " Countess of Pembroke's Arcadia "), and who was the mother of Shakespeare's dear friend. All this was denied the poet, since he had appeared upon the common stage, before the common people ; and as a player was entered in the statutes as a rogue and a vagabond ; a bar was thus placed between the two friends, to the infinite regret of both poet and patron.

Returning to the dedication, that which has puzzled

most critics is that the Earl of Pembroke, then a Knight of the Garter, should suffer merely his initials to appear with the prefix of Mr. The poems give us the solution. Sonnet 108 tells us that although the youth had then become "a man," the poet is determined to consider him as young as when first " he hallowed his fair name ;" also in the final Sonnet of the first series (126) the poet keeps his promise, and addresses him as the " lovely boy" of their first meeting, to fulfil the avowal made in Sonnet 19 that he should live ever youthful in his verse. Having shewn that Shakspeare was still addressing his friend as a juvenile even when his youth was fully past, it is evident that in the same spirit he might dedicate such poems to the same person when in riper years—poems that were to perpetuate that immortal youth which he loved to extol. Thus they are not addressed to his friend as Earl of Pembroke, but as Master William Herbert, for such he was when the poet first beheld him, and so, by the aid of the poet's pen, he will ever remain.

Having prepared the reader for the following rendering of the dedicatory inscription, I have stripped it of that form, and it will now run thus :—

"To the only begetter of these ensuing Sonnets, Master William Herbert, all happiness and that eternity promised by our ever-living poet wisheth the well-wishing adventurer in setting forth."

It may also be read thus :—

"To Master William Herbert, the only begetter of these ensuing Sonnets, the well-wishing adventurer, in setting forth, wisheth all happiness and that eternity promised by our ever-living poet."

This language, made clear, signifies that they are dedicated by the publisher to the sole inspirer of the Sonnets, and by whom alone they were begotten upon the brain of

Shakespeare. The wishing him all happiness is merely echoing the sentiments of the Sonnets, as referred to in Sonnets 6 and 37.

T. T. was a Warwickshire man.* He was an eminent bookseller of his day, and probably a friend of Shakespeare; and by his announcing himself as the "well wishing adventurer" and setter forth, meaning printer and publisher, may be inferred that the poet either gave or sold him the manuscript copy of the Sonnets. By the manner in which he describes himself as their well-wisher, desiring that the friend may get the "eternity promised by our ever-living poet," it would appear like publicly thanking the poet for it, especially as in Sonnet 21 others are condemned for writing in a similar manner for gain. If further proof is wanted of T. T. being Thomas Thorpe, and of W. H. being William Herbert, I find in the folio translation of Augustine Civitatis Dei, published in 1610, that it is dedicated to William Earl of Pembroke† by Th. Th., who can be no other than Thomas Thorpe. In both the Sonnet quarto and folio Translation the publisher dedicates the work of another. In both there is a mystery, the name of Thorpe being absent from the title-page of either, and in both in the style of the address there is something fantastical. Jonson, in 1616, dedicated his epigrams to this Earl, and insinuated that in some dedications his title had been changed, and merely a cypher used. Thorpe's dedication seems to have been a subject of ridicule to George Whither, who in

---

* *Vide* unpublished MSS. of the Rev. J. Hunter in the British Museum.
† The heading is as follows:—" To the honourable patron of muses and good mindes, Lord William Earl of Pembroke, Knight of the Honourable Order," &c.

1611 inscribes his satirical poems thus :—" G. W. wisheth himself all happiness."

As conclusive testimony that Shakespeare gave instructions to Thorpe as to the dedication, it may be seen in the especially applicable designation of " only begetter" to Mr. W. H.* Thorpe himself would never have hit upon the innermost sense of the expression. Sonnet 81 clearly denotes that Shakespeare intended to pen or dictate the dedication, though he did not intend to do so till the interval of a few years had elapsed, and the 78th to 87th Sonnets, among others, declare Herbert to be the " only begetter." They were written when others were offering poems to his friend, and the poet was looking for the time when he should publicly offer his. Thorpe could foresee that Shakespeare would gain immortality, though he appears to doubt its fulfilment in the case of W. H., the friend, on account of initials alone being given. He may have thought, like Swift, that " whatever the poets pretend, it is plain they give immortality to none but themselves;" and the poet refers in Sonnet 39 to thus, as it were, standing in his friend's light. Had Shakespeare had no actual person in view when publishing these Sonnets, he would probably have given them a fictitious name, after the manner of other publications of this sort. His contemporaries, who sonnetted lady " patronesses," did so, but as Herbert was both patron and friend, his very initials are given as a

* To those who want further conviction of the right of converting Mr. to Master, the following contemporary instances are given :—Henry Peacham to " Minerva Brittania," 1612, in addition to his name, adds his degree as follows :—" Mr. of Arts." Howell also, in his familiar letters, " Epistolæ Ho-Elianæ," frequently uses the cypher as above.

safeguard that he shall get the eternity promised. The Dedication is thus the most open of any of the Sonnet dedications of the age.

To the inquiry frequently made, whether the Sonnets were printed in their written order, or is the present arrangement merely arbitrary? I answer that unless we receive them as published in the life of the poet, as in their proper sequence, they have no meaning at all, every attempt at rearrangement having proved a total failure.

My reason for believing they are so is by internal evidence, and the relation of Sonnet to Sonnet. They are also printed like no other sonnets of the period, being arranged as consecutive stanzas,* in the manner in which Thorpe undoubtedly received them in the manuscript which Shakespeare himself wrote, and are thus printed in a very irregular manner for Sonnets, as if one continuous poem, broken up into one hundred and twenty-six divisions, some of them being partly on one page and partly on another, and with the first complete chain of Sonnets divided from the second group by a mark of separation with the pen, which Thorpe has also imitated.

Appended to them is a beautiful though quaint poem, named a "Lover's Complaint." A dejected maiden piteously laments that her lover has captivated other hearts beside her own. The poem has all the marks of being an early production, though the poet may have revised it when adding it to his Sonnet manuscript. "The fickle maid full pale" in whom, in spite of advancing age, "some beauty peeped through lattice of seared age," and

---

* Spenser, a few years before, had written several poems in the same stanza as these Sonnets.

who wished to be thought still young, having a hand
" whose white weighs down the airy scale of praise,"
seems to be no other than Queen Elizabeth, placed as a
foil to the almost fabulous beauty of a youth (probably
a portrait of her lover Leicester) who is described in the
May morn of life.   The events to which it appears to
refer may have deterred its publication until after the
Queen's death.   By its appearing with the Sonnets, Lord
Herbert may have expressed admiration of it, hence it
was offered in dedication as his.   The virgin Queen
wished to remain in ". single blessedness," or she would
probably have chosen that handsome young nobleman
who was her especial favourite for a husband, and Dudley,
upon his part, would have equally rejoiced in the alliance.*
A perusal of the poem will enable the reader to discover
many covert allusions to the Court scandal of the period
and Leicester's intrigues.   It is worthy of remark, however, that the difference between the youth of this poem
and that of the Sonnets is that the first described is of
male beauty alone, the latter portrays the united beauty
of the sexes, the male predominant.   Sexual female
loveliness is contrasted with the diviner paradisial beauty
of man, to whom is offered intellectual homage.

Prior to entering upon our subject, it may not be unin-
teresting to the reader to glance at the allusions made to
the Sonnet epistles during and after the poet's lifetime.

---

* Elizabeth is known to have received numerous gifts from her courtiers,
especially from Leicester. The maiden of the poem accepted from her
lover rich gifts.   The earl's horsemanship was such that immediately after
the Queen's accession she appointed him to the distinguished office of
Master of the Horse. This pre-eminence is extolled in several stanzas. Sir
R. Naunton says of Leicester :—" He was a very goodly person, and singular well featured, and all his youth well favoured and of a sweet aspect."

For the sake of brevity, I have omitted to insert the numerous extracts, both in prose and verse, which I had gathered, and merely give the titles of some of the principal works and the heads of their allusions, that the curious student may search for himself.

The earliest I have discovered is in Drayton's "Owl," a satirical poem, written in 1604, and published in that year. It touches upon Shakespeare's apparent humility to his young friend, as witnessed by a jealous observer. Our poet is covertly rebuked for extolling to his patron's ear "his rare perfections," the wonder of the Court (which Sonnet 1 confirms), and for loathing the means which first brought him honour; for not respecting himself or his "great profession," by bending his great mind "to the slight favour of some lord to come." This numerous Sonnets appear to bear out sufficiently far for a rival's retort. Drayton also in numerous instances throughout his poems proves himself envious of Shakespeare. Our poet, upon his part, merely makes a few satirical allusions to him and his sonnets, which were well understood in that day.

Ben Jonson, who owed so much to Shakespeare, was extremely jealous of him, and viewed him as a powerful obstacle in his own path; hence it is not strange to find that he has ridiculed our poet and his friend in several instances. Here he would find scope for his pen far more successfully than in trying to raise a laugh at Shakespeare's disregard of the unities, or in sneering at the play of the "Tempest," and calling it a drollery; though it must be said to the honour of Ben that he lived to redeem himself, and paid the highest tribute to the genius

c

of his great rival, whom he lovingly styles "gentle Shake-speare." His dislike to Sonnets, although he wrote some himself, might induce him to jest at our poet's sonnet-teering, but what he has done appears written without the least malice. However, let his motive have been what it might, in 1609 was written and printed his comedy of "Epicœne, or The Silent Woman," and I refer the reader to the scenes in which Sir John Daw and Sir Amorous La Foole appear. In these characters it will be found that Sir John Daw represents Shakespeare, and Sir Amorous La Foole Herbert, drawn to the life, as near as Jonson dared. He states in the second prologue that it gave offence, some of the characters being taken as per-sonal applications. Daw was a cant term for a lawyer, so in the First Part of King Henry VI.:—

> " But in these nice sharp quillets of the law,
> Good faith, I am no wiser than a daw."

Shakespeare, it has been assumed, at one time followed the law ; and it may have been for this reason, or for his volubility, which Jonson elsewhere decries, that induced him to apply to him this name ; but Robert Greene may have given rise to it, as he has characterised Shakespeare in his "Groat's Worth of Wit" as a daw arrayed in borrowed plumage. Daw* instances the Bible and law as most worthy of study preferable to classical authors. For this opinion he is jeered at. His common conversa-tion is said to exceed the essays of the ancients, and is worthy of record for the benefit of posterity. He desires to rise in the State, and is said to be fit to guide the

---

* And he may have styled him Sir John from Greene's designating Shake-speare as " an absolute Johannes factotum." Jonson speaks of this tract of Greene's in the play.

belm of government. To the friend Herbert the applica
tion is more direct, as the reader will discover. They
are said to be silly imitators of the friendships of antiquity, of Peliades and Orestes, Damon and Pythias, &c.
There appear in Jonson's comedy touches of character
regarding Shakespeare that are elsewhere confirmed, and
which are easily discoverable ; and to it the reader is
referred to draw his own inferences, as a complete
analysis would demand a separate article. The plot of
the play turns upon a boy whom the ladies make their
sport for his effeminacy ; they feign him to be half a
woman. Like Beatrice, they talk of dressing him in
their apparel to make him their waiting gentlewoman.
Jonson is sarcastic throughout the whole play, as is
Shakespeare through his Sonnets, upon the mystery of
woman's false adornments. Epicœne, the boy, is dressed
as a woman. Sir John Daw pretends to make love to
him as a mistress, and writes verses which are styled, in
reference to Shakespeare's first seventeen Sonnets, " A
Ballad of Procreation." (See extract from the play,
additional notes to Sonnet 1). It will be seen from the
following line in Jonson's play, edit. 1609, how he
quipped Shakespeare's shifting designation of " Master-
mistress." To this line a note is appended by one of
Jonson's ablest critics :—

" Such a rook as the other, that will betray his master to be seen."

" The rook here meant was Sir John Daw, who had no master to betray,
but he pretended to make love to Epicœne, who was to be a party at the
feast, but as she is the person intended I have made no scruple to change
the master into mistress, which alteration has also the sanction of the first
folio of his collected works in 1616."

The allusion being past, Jonson himself set the word

right ; and he also, in his " Bartholomew Fair," introduces a puppet interlude, styled " A True Trial of Friendship," between Damon and Pythias, two faithful friends of the Bankside. The worthies after quarelling about a mistress, again become fast friends, and re-appear, each with the Dunmow Flitch of Bacon. Jonson delighted in placing upon the stage those from whom he took offence ; and has been deservedly blamed for his malicious ridicule in this way of Inigo Iones, the architect. At this point will be introduced a contemporary of Shakespeare, not altogether unknown in connection with him ; as he has left some verses to and of our poet, which have kept his name from oblivion. It will be seen that this almost unknown person had closer relationship to our poet than has hitherto been suspected. It will be shown that he, and he alone, was the great unknown rival Shakespeare feigned to fear, proofs of which will be given in their proper place. All that we shall say of him at present is, that in 1611 he published a satire called the " Scourge of Folly," portions of which are inserted in this work. It was evidently written after he had received some merited homethrust from Shakespeare's pen, who rightly " brandished a lance," as Jonson hath it, " at the eyes of ignorance." He allows our poet to have wit divine, making all it touches shine with glory ; but he also charges him with debasing his great powers, by spending such treasure upon an unworthy object, to which he adds :—

> " And for an hunger starven fee, alas,
> To make an idol of a golden ass ;
> And (oh !) that ever any should record
> And chronicle the sedges of a Lord ! " &c.

Thus, in Shakespeare's words, " He misses not much—No !

he doth but mistake the truth totally." The Sonnets prove both these assertions to be wrong. Shakespeare would neither receive money nor gifts, that he might not lay himself open to this stigma, even the gift of tablets that he received from his friend (Sonnet 122), as a counter-gift to a choice volume which the poet had presented him with (Sonnet 77, at the presumed conclusion of the Sonnet poem to his friend), was given to another—there was no need of a memorandum-book to remind Shakespeare of his friend. As to the reproach contained in the preceding lines, Shakespeare answers for himself in Sonnet 105 ; and for his friend we have the testimony of Lord Clarendon, among others, that he was an honour to the age, so that Dogberry Davies must have his own epithets applied to himself, which he has in his own words :—

> " Alas !
> That ere this dotard made me such as ass
> To bear such, and that in such a thing,
> Which we call chronicle, so on me bring
> A world of shame," etc.

His satire occupies numerous pages ; and though he styles it " Paper's Complaint," it is plainly his own, but he has artfully screened his object, by mixing with it matter of an altogether contrary nature. He had undoubtedly seen the Sonnets Shakespeare had written for his friend and, either spurred by ignorance or rivalry, mistook their motives, as will be seen by the additional notes to Sonnets 78, 86. The patronage Davies was seeking was evidently denied. He exclaims :—

> " Away with patronage, a plague upon't !
> That hideous word is worse than termagant,
> Call for no aid—where none is to be found."

It is remarkable that not till Shakespeare's death did

Davies dare to address Lord Herbert again. In 1616 he dedicated a volume to him, which has become so scarce that our national collection has failed to obtain a copy. He is compelled, however, to praise Shakespeare's erection of verse for his friend. He says, with a sneer,

> " What boots such buildings to wear ages out,
> A goodly piece of work it is no doubt."

Davies takes altogether a vulgar, outward view of the Sonnets ; but he does not fail to observe his great rival's allusions to himself. He wishes for " a world of shame " to fall upon them who have so disgraced him, making his injuries historical ; and confesses he must endure it all, and ends with the consolation, that it is for his own advantage,—

> " So may ye grace me with eternal lines,
> That compass can and gage the deep'st designs."

In the same volume, " The Scourge of Folly," among the Epigrams, there is one (No. 180) referring to the same circumstance, it is entitled " Æsop, the Stage-player." In it, he relates his having once paid a visit to English Æsop.*

> " I came to English Æsop on a tide,
> As he lay tired† (as tired) before the play ;
> I came unto him in his flood of pride ;
> He then was king and thought I should obey.
> And so I did, for with all reverence, I
> As to my sovereign (though to him unknown)
> Did him approach ; but lo he cast his eye,
> As if therein I had presumption shown.

---

* The celebrated Roman actor of that name is here referred to. The comparison may have been suggested by Æsop having become rich by his profession, as Shakespeare had become wealthy by his. Davies, when speaking of Shakespeare, refers to this in these words :—" When men have become rich they are said to be made men."

† " Tired," for attired ; a quibble is here intended—Shakespeare often used the word thus.

I like a subject (with submiss regard)
Did him salute ; yet he regreeted me
But with a nod, because his speech he spared
For lords and knights that came his grace to see.
But I supposed he scorned me : by which scorn
I deemed him to be some demi-god :
(That's more than king,) at least, (what thoughts discern)
And marked my feigned fawnings with a nod !
But I well knew him (though he knew not me)
To be a player ; and for some few crowns,
Spent on a supper, any man may be
Acquainted with them from their kings to clowns.
But I (as Aaron with the golden calf)
Did gross idolatry with him commit ;
Nay, my offence was more than this by half,
He erred against his will, but I with wit :
For wit me taught : (I thought for proof of folly,)
To try conclusions with this doting ass.
I him adored too much, but he (unwholly)
Took 't on him smoothly, but well let that pass :
His golden coat his eye dimmed, I suppose,
That he could not well see my velvet hose ;
But if I e'er salute him so again,
Crown him, and cockscomb crown for my pain."

It would appear, from this narrative, that Davies obtained admission among the guests who were assembling,
probably, at the " Mermaid," and that Shakespeare was
expecting some noble personages, and appeared arrayed
in all the pomp and kingly majesty that the occasion
demanded, and as this was the character he chiefly assumed on the stage, he seemed in a region too elevated
to observe Davies's " feigned fawnings." Dekker, in his
" Gulls Horn Book," chap. 6, gives us an insight into
these meetings. He tells us " that after the play was
over, poets adjourned to supper with knights, where they
in private unfolded the secret parts of their dramas to
them."

Among Davies's Epigrams there is one to our poet,
with this heading, " To our English Terence, Mr. Will

Shakespeare." As it has connection with the foregoing, and also with the Sonnets, it is introduced here. It intimates that our poet would have attained some post at Court had he never appeared upon the stage, and that he had his detractors. It also hints that his colleagues cared not to print his plays, but jealously kept them, and became rich by them. These are his words :—

> " Some say, good Will, which I in sport do sing,
> Hadst thou, not played some kingly parts in sport
> Thou had'st been a companion for a king,
> And been a king among the meaner sort.
> Some others rail, but rail as they think fit,
> Thou hast no railing, but a reigning wit :
> And honestly thou sowest, which they do reap,
> So to increase their stock which they do keep."

This is high praise, he was not only king of wits, but eminently honest in his dealings and works. This interesting Epigram appears to have been written prior to their rivalry.

Having now shown the allusions to the Sonnets among our poet's contemporaries, those the poet himself makes are worthy of notice. Though they are, as might be expected, not made in a direct manner, a careful reader of the Sonnets cannot fail to discover them. The first in point of date is in that brilliant drama, King Henry V., which was written during the first or second year of Shakespeare's acquaintanceship with Master Herbert. In Act III, Se. 7, there are manifest allusions to his young friend in the character of the Dauphin of France. Shakespeare has depicted himself in the Duke of Orleans, and in the Constable of France appears some envious detractor, whom he has by this means ridiculed. It is not too much to say that if this scene is divested of the interest thus restored to it, it would not only be an unnecessary adjunct to the drama, but meaningless. The reader can refer to the scene, and, without further comment, discover the gist. One touch of similitude which a reader might overlook, is alone pointed out. The Dauphin brags that the mistress of his choice, *i. e.*, his horse, wears his own hair. So, in Sonnet 68, the more than mistress of Shakespeare's choice, *i.e*, his friend, is lauded for the same merit. A far nobler impersonation was reserved for Herbert as Benedick, in the delightful Comedy of "Much Ado About Nothing," which a perusal of at once testifies, and is well supported by the Rev. Joseph Hunter, in his valuable collection of notes upon Shakespeare. I shall endeavour to support, by new matter, what this gentleman adduces. The well-known military ardour of the young lord, renders these, in both plays, characteristic portraits.

The next in sequence is to be found in the serious and philosophical drama of "Measure for Measure," in which the characteristics of the later Sonnets strongly appear.[*] There is evidence to prove that this play was written in or a little prior to 1603, which is precisely the date Sonnets 78 to 126 were written. It will presently be shown that Shakespeare performed the character of the Duke of Vicenzio, and the meditative duke is, in fact, a dramatic portrait of Shakespeare himself. My reason for believing that he appeared in this character upon the stage, is from the circumstance of D'Avenant's drama " The Law against

---

[*] All the principal passages being profound, involved, and more or less obscure.

Lovers," containing the following remarkable passage, referring to him as the Duke. D'Avenant in the above-named play, has blended together " Much Ado About Nothing " and " Measure for Measure," when speaking of Marion's seculsion at the ' Moated Grange,' and the habit in which the Duke conceals himself for her advantage, as if to chronicle the fact that Shakspeare had taken the character, he says, " She has been advised by a bald dramatic poet of the next cloister ;" and Lucio, in the original play, repeatedly sneers at the friar's baldness.

As announced, it is the purpose of these pages to show that the Sonnets under consideration were written with a satirical motive, to bring into ridicule mistress sonnetting It is obvious that some of the sonnetteers of the time would feel offended. Drayton and Davies, both industrious writers of this species of verse, leave signs of being so. The next largest writer of Sonnets was Habington. He dedicated to Castara in 1630 a volume of praise. She was a lady of high birth whom he married. He styles her " The Diety of her Sex." His Sonnets are divided into three poems. The first part is addressed to her as his mistress ; the second part when he was possessed of her in marriage ; and the third part dwells upon religious contemplations. Among them are these lines, levelled at some poet who had given him some offence :—

> " If this man please
> His silly patron with hyperboles
> Or most mysterious nonsense, give his brain
> But the strappado in some wanton strain."

This appears to refer to no other than Shakespeare, whom Habington wishes to see lashed in a like manner to that in which Shakspeare had ridiculed him and others, in what Habington aptly calls a work of mystic ideas and exaggeration.

Shakespeare's Sonnets seem not to have been in much request in the life-time of the poet, except amongst the few "private friends," they being of too enigmatical a nature for the general public ; and it was not till 1640, twenty-four years after his death, and ten years after that of his patron friend, that a second edition appeared. This edition was altogether in a different form ; it had then blended with it the "Passionate Pilgrim" and the songs from the Plays. It was compiled by John Benson, and printed by Thomas Cotes, the printer of the second folio of our author's dramatic works, 1632. The poems are arranged in little groups, the original sequence being broken up, and even the closest connected Sonnets are separated. The whole is, in fact, rearranged, or rather disarranged. The groups have headings, such as the " Glory of Beauty," " A Masterpiece," " Loss and Gain," " Love's Cruelty," &c. He places first the 67th and 68th, as if to indicate that the collection was of a satirical nature, and to denote unmistakably the sex addressed, which in these instances is especially revealed, as it is in other Sonnets purposely concealed. He has also omitted to insert the 18th, 19th, 43rd, 56th, 75th, and 76th. His object in selecting these for expulsion is obviously on account of Shakespeare having in these instances not only frequently repeated the thoughts of other Sonnets, but almost the very words also. These omissions appear not to have been detected hitherto, on account of his arrangement being unnumbered. The line in Sonnet 108, which stands thus in the original :—

> " Nothing, sweet boy ; and yet like prayers divine,"

is altered to

> " Nothing, sweet love, and yet like prayers divine."

But that which is most singular is his Preface to the Reader, which has never been reprinted, and is as follows :—

" To THE READER.

" I here presume, under favour, to present to your view some excellent and sweetly composed poems of Master William Shakespeare, which in themselves appear of the same purity the author himself, then living, avouched. They had not the fortune, by reason of their infancy in his death, to have the due accommodation of proportionable glory with the rest of his everliving works. Yet the lines will afford you a more authentic approbation than my assurance any way can to invite your allowance ; in your perusal you shall find them serene, clear, and elegantly plain,—such gentle strains as shall recreate and not perplex your brain. No intricate or cloudy stuff to puzzle intellect, but perfect eloquence, such as will raise your admiration to his praise. This assurance will not differ from your acknowledgments, and certain I am my opinion will be seconded by the sufficiency of these ensuing lines. I have been somewhat solicitous to bring this forth to the perfect view of all men, and in so doing glad to be serviceable for the continuance of glory to the deserved author in these his poems."

There appears something ironical in this. It is the reverse, not only as to the Sonnets, but also to Shakespeare's opinion of what this species of verse should be, as when extolling them he applies to them the epithet " deep-brained," not only as their characteristic, but their highest merit.

Benson appends a poem to the preface, which gives testimony that they were the known effusions of the poet's mature years. The bard is thus addressed :—

> " These learned poems amongst thine after birth
> That makes thy name immortal on the earth."

Both the laudatory lines and the irreconcileable preface,

from which the above are taken, exhibit plainly that not
only the general public, but also the personal acquaint-
ances of Shakespeare were mystified. It is a curious
piece of information that the author, when living, vindicated the poems : that he upon some occasions avouched
their purity, possibly from the attacks of those who only
condemned that which they had not understood. Benson,
it is evident, could not understand them ; this led him to
break the poem up into parts, which makes the matter
worse ; but viewing them as pure, crediting Shakespeare's
testimony, he feigns to see them so. It is somewhat to
our theory that we arrive at the same conclusion Shakespeare himself avouched, and to which his life bore testimony.

The question now arises why Benson omitted the Dedication, broke up the poems into such complete disorder,
and caused by inappropriate headings such general con-
fusion. The solution is that he did not understand them,
nor did he know any other who did. He might have
known, if only from hearsay, that they were dedicated to
Lord Herbert in the poet's life-time, but how to apply the
contents to either poet or patron was past his comprehen-
sion. Lord Herbert, at this date, had been dead ten
years, and with him the secret : to have introduced the
Dedication again would have been the height of impropriety, or even to mention it, after having confounded its
application. He hoped, as others have since done, by
ignoring the Dedication and destroying the continuity, to
pass the poems off as the essence of simplicity ; but
words are words, and can only be explained by the right
explanation.

Joshua Poole, in 1677, appears the next who sought by
alteration to convey a different meaning. In the above
year he published his " English Parnassus." In the compilation he made numerous extracts from the Plays of
Shakespeare, and also inserted many passages from the
Sonnets, which he headed with titles, and the passages
themselves are altered. In this particular he went a step
beyond the 1640 editor. To the extracts from the
first five Sonnets he gives the title of the " Resolved
Fair Virgin," totally disregarding that Shakespeare meant
bachelor ; the sex is altered from " him " and " his " to
" her" and " she."

INTRODUCTION.

" His was an age of fantastic conceits, and he more or less partook of its spirit."—*Ferguson's Hist. of England*, p. 140, *Article on Shakespeare.*

The Sonnets have been objected to on account of their being filled with fantastical conceits. They are pictures for and of the age. In this burlesque Shakespeare has not only used the conceits, but also purposely imitated the style of others, and while doing so, emulated to surpass them in their own sphere. As it was the custom for Sonnetteers to use biblical expressions, Shakespeare in imitation of them has also used them, so that it was not on account of his being fortunate enough to find that rarity, a true friend, that led him to lavish such excesses in his verse ; for the object of these excesses, as will be proved, was parody. He did find such a friend, who excelled, he asserts, the female friends of other poets ; one to whom he might exclaim, with his own philosophical Hamlet :—

> " Since my dear soul was mistress of her choice,
> And could of men distinguish, her election
> Hath seal'd thee for herself."

And it is but natural to suppose that, having found such a friend, he would speak in high terms of him, as he was

devoted to his interests, of high birth, and had a growing
power at Court ; whereas our poet's earliest patron, Lord
Southampton, had no interest whatever, and appeared
always in disgrace, was a man with a temper soon ruffled,
and was not outwardly endowed by nature with the rare
personal attractions of our poet's patron and dearest
friend of the Sonnets, that friend whom he passionately
tells us was more lovely and temperate than a summer's
day, and from whom radiated all the beauty of the
world. This is particularly alluded to in an alliterative
line of the 20th Sonnet. With two such friends in close
unity, the one graced by Nature with rare mental beauty
within, the other as rich in outward show—so that each
possess alike as it were two natures, the one the mental
graces of the sexes, the other their external beauty—it is
not surprising that such a poet should eulogise such a
friend, even for Shakespeare, the most sparing of all poets
in writing panegyrics on any one. But it is the warmth
of this friendship, and the excessively amorous language
used to express the passion, that has ever been a stumbling
block to critics ; they never observed that the drift of the
poet was parody. The plea has been made that such was
the custom of the time, and it must be granted that there
are instances where similar utterances are used, though they
are rare and moderate in comparison, for there is nothing
of such length and power or personal application. The
only parallel examples which I have met with will be
given.

The religion of Love and Beauty were themes which
had engaged the pens of the divinely chaste Dante and
Petrarch, the one addressing Beatrice as a religious

symbol, the other Laura, both married ladies. But the writer whom Shakespeare most resembles, by accident, not design, is the great Michael Angelo, who, in this species of verse, penned magnificent hymns to the Marchioness of Pescara,* a lady to whom he appears to have offered a devoted platonic friendship : his chaste love of the beautiful is exalted to religion. Of a like colossal mind with Shakespeare, it is remarkable that in other moods and motives he is the only sonnetteer to be compared with him. From the foregoing and other eminent examples which might be adduced, it appears to have been the custom for the Sonnet to turn upon either illegal or futile attachments. This throws further light upon Shakespeare's Sonnets, showing them to be, as will be seen, of the nature of parodies ; for a particular instance see the 20th Sonnet, which is the key to the whole series. As to Dante and Petrarch, they evidently choose married ladies as symbols, their love not being carnal, but divine. With love and beauty Shakespeare combines friendship, and pours forth his praises to a man, as being worthier than the mistresses of other poets, his cheek being adorned with nature's own rose of truth, the seat and emblem of beauty.

Richard Barnefield, in 1595, wrote a poem, which he styled "The Affectionate Shepherd," in a somewhat similar strain, but without the "deep-brained" subtleness and fantastic caprices which are to be found in every line of the Sonnets. Master Herbert, who loved praise to an

---

* The Sonnets of Michael Angelo, beautifully written in the author's own handwriting, are still preserved among the treasures of the Vatican library, but of Shakespeare's whole writings not one line is known to exist.

excess that even Shakespeare reproached him for, may
have expressed his admiration for this style of composition, and hence our poet so moulded his verse, seeing
that it would afford him scope to exercise his fancy.
Barnefield's poem details the passion of a shepherd for a
beautiful boy, and is, as he states, a harmless imitation of
Virgil's second Eclogue, "Corydon and Alexis," for which,
in spite of the plea he made, and the vindications made
by some poetical advocates who took up his cause, he met
with considerable censure. It is, he declares, his first
poem, being written when but a young man, and is
indeed the essence of Arcadian innocence and simplicity.
It went through several editions, and became very popu-
lar ; but as the author had no higher object in view than
to please, it bears only a slight resemblance to the Sonnet-
poems Shakespeare afterwards penned, though he appears
to have imitated the following portion of the " Affectionate Shepherd " when claiming Master Herbert's loving
friendship (Sonnet 20). In Barnefield's poem the old
shepherd thus addresses the beautiful boy :—

> " Compare the love of fair Queen Gwendolom*
> With mine, and thou shalt find how she doth love thee.
> I love thee for thy qualities divine,
> She doth love another swain above thee ;
> I love thee for thy gifts, she for her pleasure ;
> I for thy virtues, she for beauty's treasure."

But here all resemblance ends. Shakespeare had neither
the Latin poet nor his own petty contemporary in
view ; the Sonnet writing of the day was the mark he
aimed at.

In Shakespeare's Dramas there are several expressions of

---

* A princess of great beauty, mentioned by romantic writers.

a parallel tendency to the most endearing in his Sonnets. It is of the friendship of Aufidius for Coriolanus that a servant exclaims :—

"Our general himself makes a mistress of him."

Again :—

"I tell thee, fellow, thy general is my lover."

Guiderius also bears the same loving emotions in his breast toward the supposed boy Fidele. He exclaims :—

"Were you a woman, youth,
I should woo hard."

In the same spirit, and also referable to the same Sonnet, its counterpart, it is said of Hermione :—

"Women will love her that she is a woman
More worth than any man ; men that she is
The rarest of all women."

Cowley, in a poem upon platonic love, thus defines the passion :—

"I thee both as a man and woman prize,
For a perfect love implies
Love in all capacities."

Shirley, the last of the Shakespearian school of dramatists, also expresses a like sentiment. It is to be found in the first edition of his poems, published in 1646. It has this heading and title :—

"'Et longum Formose Vale.'
'FRIENDSHIP,
"Or verses sent to a lover in answer of a copy which had been sent in praise of his mistress."

The poem is, as the Latin quotation expresses, a farewell to a beautiful woman. The argument is precisely the same as Shakespeare uses. The youth is told that though the lady he adores—

> " Include the graces of fair womankind,
> I shall not think her worth my praise or smile,
> And yet I have a mistress all this while,
> But am a convert from that sex, and can,
> Reduced to my discretion, love a man
> With honor and religion ; such a one
> As dares be singly virtuous 'gainst the town."

After extolling his graces and accomplishments, he concludes thus :—

> " Then and the wonder right ; he is young, too,
> As handsome as thy mistress, more divine,
> And hath no fault but that I call him mine.
> My jealousy doth cloud his name, 'tis fit,
> Nor art thou ripe for thy conversion yet."

It is evident from these examples that the old poets loved to compare strong friendship to wedded love, as a marriage of mind betwixt man and man, a wedlock of the purest type. But Shakespeare went further ; he consummates this alliance by an allegorical marriage of his friend to his Muse.

I have now shown the important position friendship held in society, and the chivalrous laws demanded to uphold it, the loving qualities it imposed, and its perfection, worthy of triumph, when mature years grafted its love and wisdom on youthful beauty ennobled by birth, and the pure platonic love offered with such full soul from friend to friend ; which love was then extolled as virtuous, dignified, and sublime, even to religion, such as gave grace to the mystery of poetry and beauty. From the foregoing passage it is obvious that such writing must not be judged by malicious interpretation, or the writers accused of crime such as their souls abhorred. Shakespeare has left testimony, if such was needed, of his detestation of such grievous depravity in his " Troilus

and Cressida," in which a character so accused is denounced with the bitterest reproaches. But I contend,
and can prove beyond doubt, that the entire Sonnets are
a satire upon the reigning custom of mistress-sonnetting,
and by a curious coincidence they were penned just
at the time Cervantes was writing his inimitable
satirical burlesque on the romancists.

In conclusion, and to support this view relative to the
purity of Shakespeare's Sonnets, Dryden, when drawing a
comparison between Shakespeare and Fletcher, observes:—
" He excelled in the more manly passions, Fletcher in the
softer; Shakespeare writ better betwixt man and man,
Fletcher betwixt men and women; consequently the one
described friendship better, the other love. Yet Shakespeare taught Fletcher to write love, and Juliet and Des-
demona are originals. It is true the scholar had the
softer soul, but the master had the kinder. Friendship
is both a passion and a virtue essentially; love is a
passion only in its nature, and is not a virtue but by
accident; good nature makes friendship, but effeminacy
love."

With these hints of explanation we are brought to the
unfolding of the Sonnets, which is the aim and end of
these pages. Before commencing, the reader is requested
never to lose sight of the poet's ultimate drift in his
progress through the lengthened chain of conceits and
hyperbolical metaphors with which these poems abound.
It will be found there are three different sections or
undercurrents of purpose:—

First, that the whole set of Sonnets are satires upon
mistress-sonnetting, and upon the sonnetteers of Shake-

speare's day, and that Drayton first, but afterwards
Davies, were more directly the subjects of his sportive
musings and feignings.

Second, and more important, that they are autobiogra-
phical, containing much that is valuable.

Third, and which is of itself the key that unlocks the
heart of the mystery, is the conceit of Shakespeare having
united his muse to his friend by marriage of verse and
mind ; by which means and for which favour his youth
and beauty are immortalised, but which theme does not
fully commence till the friend had declined the invitation
to marriage, which refusal begets the mystic melody.

The inference from the Sonnets and Dedication is that
they were written at the especial request of the friend
who, in spite of all expostulation, was so self-willed as
not to be denied. Hence Shakespeare poured his whole
soul into the task of developing the romantic youth's
fantastic caprice, and the whole turns upon this pivot.
The youth sought and obtained Shakespeare's friendship ;
for reasons before stated the poet persuades him to marry,
but without effect. The Comedy of " Much Ado about
Nothing " was then (1599) written to show how such
another military-minded, self-willed bachelor was trapped
at last. Returning to the Sonnets, we find the youth
declining the invitation to marry and preserve his youth
and beauty by children. To effect this object, Shakespeare
marries the youth to his immortal verse, which binds
them together in wedded friendship, so that the poet, in
his unadulterous love, permits him to become " the onlie
begetter of these insuing Sonnets," which perpetuate his
youth and beauty and their loving friendship in ever-

living verse. Finally, the poet viewed his lengthy chain of Sonnet stanzas as his masterpiece, upon which to build his reputation and undying fame, exclaiming :—

> " Not marble, nor the gilded monuments
> Of princes, shall outlive this powerful rhyme."

Which he himself fully believed, though the vaunt was a strain beyond his usual humility, his object being to ape the bombast of the sonnetteers, and at the same time excel them.

THE ARGUMENT.

"Some critics, or I'm much deceiv'd, will ask,
What means this wild, this allegoric masque ?
Beyond all bounds of truth this author shoots
'Tis idle stuff!—And yet I'll prove it true."
Epilogue spoken at a revival of Comus.

" Choose one of two companions for thy life,
Then be as true as thou would'st have thy wife ;
Though he lives joyless that enjoys no friend,
He that hath many pays for't in the end."
William, Earl of Pembroke's poems.

" I never mean to wed,
That torture to my bed ;
My muse is she,
My love shall be."
" If I a poem have, that poem is my son."
Randolph's poems.

The poem opens with the praise of a beautiful youth
and the desire that that youth should speedily marry and
beget offspring. The poet at once strikes at the root of
human existence, as a tendency to farther the operation of
that law which the Creator impressed on our first parents,
" Be fruitful and multiply." Shakespeare's wish was fulfilled, for within a few mouths after the final Sonnet (the
126th) was penned, his dear friend, Lord Herbert, was
married. This took place on the 17th of September, 1603,
and was not like the ensuing, an allegorical verse marriage,
but a matter of fact reality.

The poet had an especial purpose in commencing with these persuasions, they are a plea for much of the singular writing which follows. For, had Herbert complied, and Shakespeare still addressed his young friend, the theme, as the poet denotes, would have taken a different turn. The young friend is to alter his single state in the prime of youth, and his beauty is thus to be preserved for the admiration of posterity. This theme occupies the first seventeen Sonnets. The two following promise to preserve the youth ever youthful, in case this counsel may fail to effect the desired purpose. Nature is said to have become enamoured of the youth as she wrought him, and, as if by her example, Shakespeare becomes so too. In this ecstacy of platonic love, and as a conclusion to the foregoing Argument, Sonnet 20 is composed, in the vein in which the sportive Mercutio would have indulged. Master Herbert is styled his "master mistress" in the sense of the more than mistress of his love. This and the five following complete the declaration. As verse is used in Sonnets 18 and 19 for the aid of the youth, it is now used for the poet's own purpose. By it a mutual alliance is formed between friend and friend; and against all impediments this marriage of true minds remained inviolate (Sonnets 105 and 116). Shakespeare had a high, even a religious opinion of friendship. This is seen in all his writings. Friendship he conceived a kind of marriage, and marriage a kind of friendship, both as being made for life, and being subject to the same laws. In this particular he but entertains the same notion as philosophers of all ages and countries, both sacred and secular, both ancient and modern, of which numerous instances will be given. But it is the singular method of conducting, describing, and expressing it which has confounded all readers, no one having delved to its root, and observed from whence all the divers ramifications spring, and for what object, or they would have seen that a covert satire was begun and ended, and the poet's ultimate object accomplished.

Henceforth it is the poet's resolve to watch over his young friend with especial regard, not only with the eye of a faithful friend (82), but with the delight of an aged father over his dear child (37, 108, 126), and also with the jealous love of a husband over a young wife (93), picturing his love by the emotions of each. By observing these hints, which the poet has given us, the numerous difficulties instantly vanish, and we can discover that what would otherwise be a serious matter is but the effusion of the poet's mind when he is in a sportive mood. The peculiar situation he is placed in by the caprices of his friend, occasions him to rejoice in the consequent subtleties, with all the humour and power of which he was master. The song of Sonnets is thus an allegorical marriage between the faithful loving friends, and a parody upon the romantic attachments formed by Sonnetteers. We have the testimony of Lord Clarendon that the Earl of Pembroke was of a pleasant and facetious humour, and a disposition affable, generous, and magnificent, — which the life and poems of Lord Herbert testify.

Having removed the drapery and cast aside the mask,

an analysis of each Sonnet will be entered upon, and Shakespeare will be revealed, both as a poet and a friend. In his own words the reader will discover,

> " In him a pleuitude of subtle matter,
> Applied to cautels* all strange forms receives."

Before ending this Argument, it should be observed that as the poet and the muse are but one, yet a distinct division, so by turns they speak in unity and in division. Sometimes the poet addresses the friend in his own name, and sometimes in the name of his muse, and at other times the poet and his muse speak but as one ; and because of the friend's dual nature, he is also spoken of as the poet's more than mistress and his dearest friend, and also as the only beloved of his most loving muse. The mistress has also a twofold representation—firstly, upon the assumption of the one-ness of the friend, she is described as fair in beauty and in actions ; secondly, viewing her as she truly was, the mistress alone of the friend, and the cheater of the poet's muse, she is pictured dark in feature and darker in her deeds.

It is thought a table showing the various groups as they stand throughout the poems would be useful to the reader for easy reference. The theme of each division is also given, showing the several sections blending into an harmonious whole.

---

* Cunning designs.

THE TABLE.

IN PRAISE OF MARRIAGE.

Group 1—Sonnets 1, 2, 3, 4, 5, 6, 7, 8, 9, 10, 11, 12, 13, 14.

To his friend, persuading him to marry and beget offspring, so that a memorial of his youth and beauty may be preserved.

Group 2—Sonnets 15, 16, 17.

To fully effect this object he complies with his young friend's desire, which is to preserve his youth and beauty in verse; the while he bids him fulfil nature's law as the surest preservative, and that one might bear witness to the other.

Group 3—Sonnets 18, 19.

His friend will consent to no other alliance except that of verse, and desires to beget Sonnets, to which the poet consents, and, as it would appear, only upon the strictest terms of marriage law. If there are laws made to preserve beauty by the one means, why not by the other? Why should breach of promise be allowed for the one, and not for the other? For the honour of the marriage of his muse the poet makes this claim.

THE MARRIAGE ALLEGORY.

Group 4—Sonnets, 20, 21, 22.

The allegorical marriage commences. The friend to whom this verse is devoted is depicted of the highest beauty; the marriage of true minds is consummated, and its conditions ordained.

Group 5—Sonnets 23, 24, 25.

A plea is made for departure, and the mutual benefit of the connection proclaimed.

Group 6—Sonnets 26, 27, 28.

Departure—the resolve, and its results.

Group 7—Sonnets 29, 30, 31, 32.

The benefit of absence, the exchange of loves, censure of the unworthiness of his verse as a plea for absence.

Group 8—Sonnets 33, 34, 35.

Blaming and forgiving his friend for violating during absence the conditions of their romantic attachment.

Group 9—Sonnets 36, 37, 38, 39.

Though separated by absence, they are united by verse, by which each partakes of the other's graces and defects.

Group 10—Sonnets 40, 41, 42.

The friend is lovingly censured for his fault, which is proved a mutual advantage.

Group 11—Sonnet 43.

Though he sees the shadow of his friend in dreams by night, it does not suffice, he desires to see his loving form during the day.

Group 12—Sonnets 44, 45.

His thoughts are ever going to and returning from his friend; he wishes that he had himself the like celerity.

Group 13—Sonnets 46, 47.

A contention between the eye and the heart for loving supremacy, and a league taken between them.

Group 14—Sonnet 48.

Absence may occasion the severest loss.

Group 15—Sonnet 49.

The friend may despise in maturer years the conceit of friendship he had formed in his youth.

Group 16—Sonnets 50, 51.

The journey the while is still continued; the horse on which he rides partakes of the rider's desire to return.

Group 17—Sonnet 52.

As the four seasons of the year are blessed for being rare, so their meetings will be.

Group 18—Sonnet 53.

The friend is the beauty of the world and lovingly constant.

Group 19—Sonnet 54.

His rose appears the more beautiful for the truth of its sweetness within, and colour without.

Group 20—Sonnet 55.

The poet's verses shall prove worthy of immortalizing such excellencies.

Group 21—Sonnets 56, 57, 58.

The weariness of absence from a beloved friend; love's avowal since departure of entire submissiveness.

Group 22—Sonnets 59, 60.

Ancient poets have praised beauty. Did their praise
exceed his, or does time remain unchanged ?

Group 23—Sonnets 61, 62.

The poet sees the friend only in dreams in the night,
but others see him himself in the day time ; nevertheless, though farthest, the poet is nearest.

AN INTERIM.

The poet, for reasons explained in another place,
ceases writing till his return.

Group 24—Sonnets 63, 64, 65.

On his return, the poet commences a series of self-con-
templations. Reflections are made upon himself,
and what he has witnessed of change during absence,
and the war with time is renewed.

Group 25—Sonnets 66, 67, 68.

He is weary of witnessing the corruptions of the time
present, and satirises the then time of profaned
beauty.

Group 26—Sonnets 69, 70.

He, in part, admits that during his absence his friend
has laid himself open to slander ; by mixing with
others he is blamed with them ; their vile misjudg-
ments are censured, and their slanders imputed to
the corruptions of the times.

Group 27—Sonnets 71, 72, 73, 74.

The friend also, upon his part, esteems the poet's
worth ; the poet wills his works to him, and desires
that after his death the friend will preserve these
poems as memorials of their friendship, not so much

for their merit, as his love, it being his very spirit, is the best of gifts, and thus bringing the song to an end he consigns it to its only begetter.

Group 28—Sonnet 75.

The friend is the soul of the poet's existing thoughts.

Group 29—Sonnet 76.

Reasons given for not having varied the song, and for discontinuing it.

Group 30—Sonnet 77.

In conclusion, he is now desired to do his part, especially to improve his mind, for which purpose a volume is presented to him, with additional waste leaves, upon which he is to nurse the children of his brain, and thus enchance the value of his own worth and the book.

AN INTERIM.

Group 31—Sonnets, 78, 79, 80, 81, 82, 83, 84, 85, 86.

Renewal ; rivalry with poets for continued possession : the friend praised and blamed, and the rivals defeated.

Group 32—Sonnets, 87, 88, 89, 90, 91, 92, 93, 94, 95, 96.

The poet offers to dissolve the friendship, and free the friend from the ties which bind them ; and should the friend will it, never mention him or it any more.

Group 33—Sonnets 97, 98, 99.

Rivalry and upbraiding are ended ; the past absence it deplored ; the sweet musings it occasioned are cited in the most loving language, as a plea for faster binding their friendship.

Group 34—Sonnets 100, 101, 102, 103.

A reawakening of his Muse, excusing her having been silent, reminding his friend of the farewell request in the 77th Sonnet, and of her inability to do more to advance her ultimate object : the while attesting the silent growth of his love, hence, from now the poet speaks mostly of himself.

Group 35—Sonnets, 104, 105, 106, 107, 108.

A recapitulation, and the promised immortality of youth re-asserted and assured by the poet from this time, addressing him as not of the present but of the past.

Group 36—Sonnets, 109, 110, 111, 112, 113, 114, 115, 116, 117.

Excusing and palliating the absence of the past, and vindicating the constancy of his poetical marriage of mind to mind.

Group 37—Sonnets 118, 119.

The absence proved by comparison of natural circumstances a mutual benefit.

Group 38—Sonnets 120, 121, 122.

The faults on each side condemned, and a tender of mutual forgiveness requested. The poet vindicates his character from the charges of his calumniators, and the parting with a gift received from the friend proved to his credit.

Group 39—Sonnets 123, 124, 125.

A final protestation, constancy triumphantly attested, and his calumniators upbraided.

L'ENVOY.

Group 40—Sonnet 126.

To the friend, as the youth of the past, in proof of the
victory of verse over time.

ADDITIONAL SONNETS TO THE MISTRESS,

Being a continuation of the allegorical marriage, by which
the poet claims her as his alone, though she is alone the
friend's ; they being but one, he is hers, and she is his,
which occasions him to address her sometimes as his own
alone, and at other times to divide the poscession of her
with his friend, then, again, to assert an entire claim. This
scheme gives the widest scope to his satire, which is now
his chief aim and end.

Group 1—Sonnet 127

A satire upon what Lord Herbert terms "painted
women." By the oneness of Shakespeare and his
friend, the poet, assumes that the mistress is his own.

Group 2—Sonnet 128.

A playful conceit. He envies and would change his
state with Jacks, the keys of the instrument she
plays upon, so that he might, as they do, kiss her
hands.

Group 3—Sonnet 129.

The miseries of evil passion anatomised ; a picture of
their mutual guilt, the sin of sinful loving.

Group 4—Sonnet 130.

An ironical description of the mistress.

Group 5—Sonnets 131, 132.

A satirical picture of the mistress, whose deeds are
declared to be darker than her dark complexion.

THE UNITY DIVIDED AND AGAIN UNITED.

Group 6—Sonnets 133, 134.

Referring to Groups 8 and 10 of the series to the friend. In these the christian names of the friends are sported with, and the wilfulness of their mutual wilful loving. The poet pleads that his love suit should be lawfully accepted, and that being the friend, she is his, and he is hers.

Group 7—Sonnets 135, 136.

A continuation of the foregoing.

Group 8—Sonnet 137.

A satire upon the eye and heart's misjudgment. He returns to the oneness, and, as she is his, blames her for turning her eyes to another.

Group 9—Sonnet 138.

He views himself as the young friend, and assumes she believes so too, for which mutual flattery he makes apology.

Group 10—Sonnets 139, 140, 141.

A satire upon the thraldom of sinful loving ; he excuses her, though she is his, for turning her eyes aside. She should not do so, lest he should go mad He is mad to love one so unlovely and unloving.

Group 11—Sonnet 142.

Upon adulterous love ; mutual upbraiding of each other for the like loving faults ; she seeking the friend's love, for which he will seek her love.

THE UNITY DIVIDED.

Group 12—Sonnet 143.

He will forgive her for pursuing with loving looks another, so that other is his other self, and desires that she may gain that which she seeks if she turns her eyes to him, as he is her own loving Will.

Group 13—Sonnet 144.

The poet fears woman will allure his friend from him, and dissolve the friendship, and sever him from the poet's Muse, to whom he is virtuously allied.

AN INTERIM.

Upon the poet's return, the division made one.

Group 14—Sonnet 145.

A playful conceit; her love is hate, and her hate love.

Group 15—Sonnet 146.

The mistress apostrophises her soul; she derides herself for having sought to revive her fading beauty by painting and cost, and finally bids her soul " buy terms divine," and defeat death ere death defeats it.

Group 16—Sonnets 147, 148, 149, 150, 151, 152.

Continuing the satire upon sinful loving, and a palliation and condemnation of their mutual loving faults. Though, upon his own part, he may and does boldly affirm that his conscience cannot accuse him of unlawfully loving the love of another, as he assumes himself to be that other.

CONCLUSION.

Group 17—Sonnets 153. 154.

A variation of a fanciful conceit, alluding to his absence and love sickness. He pays the mistress a compliment, and finally assumes her to be his own.

THE EXPLANATION

OF THE

SONNETS.

"The love of man to woman is a thing common and of course, but the friendship of man to man infinite and immortal."—*Allot.*

"Friendship ought to resemble the love between man and wife, that is, two bodies to be made one will and affection."—*Meres.*

"To see two hearts that have been twined together,
Married in friendship, to the world two wonders."
Fletcher.

Sonnet 1.—The object of the verse is at once addressed as the personification of beauty—its rose, its quintessence. His friend is beheld by the exalted mental eye of the poet as creation's masterpiece, Heaven's image. The youth is told that it is the desire of all that the most beautiful of either sex should become self-renewed, and that he, a new ornament of the world, the object of general attraction, should not live and die in single blessedness,* robbing the world of his image, and sacri-

---

* Herbert appears, like Benedick, to have foolishly vowed that he would die a bachelor. See Preliminary Remarks and Additional Notes to Sonnet 10.

ficing himself and his posterity.   In this first Sonnet, to
the whole which follow, Herbert's eyes are particularly
alluded to, and the allusions are repeated throughout the
series.   We shall show that Shakespeare was not alone in
praising them.

Sonnet 2.—In an indirect manner the poet contrasts
himself with his friend, and depicts himself as deeply
marked by time,* as a foil to set off the beauty of his
friend.   In this Sonnet there is evident allusion made to
the poet's son Hamnet, who died in 1596 at the age of
twelve.   Master Herbert appears to have filled his place
in the poet's heart.

Sonnet 3.—The youth, who appears mostly to have
resembled his mother, is bid to see himself, when in
years, in his children's eyes, as his mother sees herself in
his, in the April of her years, young and beautiful.†

Sonnet 4.—As Nature so freely gave to him, he should
be as bounteous to others; if not, her gifts will be
buried with him.

Sonnet 5.—Time, that has made him the gaze of all
eyes, will destroy all his beauties.   He is therefore desired
to preserve the pride of his summer, even as in winter
are kept the sweets of summer flowers.

Sonnet 6.—He is bid, ere his beauties are marred by

---

* In those days this would not appear strange, men frequently being
called old, and even aged, when they had but passed the freshness of their
first youth.

† There are several points of resemblance in these persuasions, and in
' Much Ado about Nothing," to a little work on letter-writing by N.
Breton, of which editions appeared between 1595 and 1609, more especially
to a letter persuading to marry, and the answer.

the winter of age, to find a preservative, to seek some
phial worthy to contain such a treasure, that it may not
become self-destroyed. If he fails to do so, the result of
his self-will is pictured in

Sonnet 7, in a majestic comparison between the rising
and setting of the sun, and the course youth runs
towards declining and decrepid age.

Sonnet 8.—The youth, whose voice is as music, loves
to receive the poet's verses, but is averse to the theme
they contain. The Sonnet, the bard's harp, is said to
have strings, referring to the rhyming verses in married
unison. It is thus intimated that the Sonnet is a piece
of music as well as poetry.

Sonnet 9.—The delicate youth is demanded his reason
for desiring to live a single life. Is it for fear " of wetting
a widow's eye?" If he dies without issue, not one person only but the whole world will lament his loss. This,
coupled with the fact of Herbert being of a delicate
nature, proves it not of ironical tendency. Beatrice says
to Benedick, " I heard you were in a consumption."

Sonnet 10.—It is to his shame, being beloved by all, to
love none. The poet adds :—" But marry," if only for
" the love of me."

Sonnet 11.—Others, without his graces, may barrenly
perish ; but he, being Nature's richest stamp, was not
made for himself alone, but to print more. Him she has
richest endowed, by forming him of a bi-sexual nature.
(See Sonnets 20, 53, and 59, in which this idea is
expressed.)

Sonnet 12.—As time destroys all things, there is no means of withstanding his ravages but by offspring. It is the friend who is the emblem of the

> " Violet in the youth of primy nature,
> Forward, not permanent, sweet, not lasting."

Sonnet 13.—Not being made for himself alone, he should prepare to give himself up, and as he had a father, let his son say so, implying that he had a beginning and will have an ending ; he was begotten, and should beget.

Sonnet 14.—There is no need for consulting the stars, as it is self-evident that if he neglects the poet's advice there will be an end both to him and of him.

Sonnet 15.—The poet meditates upon the mutability of all things : that men, like plants, increase, like them flourish and die ; and that his friend's fair flower and the blossoms which may spring from it are alike doomed to bloom and wither. Hence he wishes to graft his beauty to undying flowers of Parnassus, and set them afresh in the garden of his Muse. As time will darken the brightness of his friend, the poet will make war with him, and will at once begin, ere the heyday of his beauty shall have passed away, and this task he will accomplish out of pure love.

Sonnet 16.—The friend is again demanded his reason for not using surer and more fruitful means of guarding against decay than by verse. Why desire to become wedded to his barren rhyme ? He has now attained to the summit of life's golden age, and many virgins virtuously desire to bear him living flowers, much nearer his resemblance than the verse can portray ; for by children his life would be renewed, and he would still live in men's eyes, not drawn in the poet's lifeless lines, but in living lines of nature ; for the poet's imperfect pen* can neither show his outward beauty nor his inward worth, but by giving himself to another he may preserve both ; and though the poet's pen may be the best pencil of the time that can trace his beauty, yet as in Sonnets 101 and 103, it quite fails in picturing the perfection of his living face.   In the next this verse-portrait is again referred to.

Sonnet 17.—A final request is made, and a final reason given, why he should follow the poet's advice. He is told the next generation will disbelieve the verse, even though filled with his own just praise. The beauty of his eyes alone is past the poet's power of expression, and could he recount all his graces in fresh verse, the next age would discredit the divineness of his perfections, and his just deserts would be despised as the lies of an old frenzied poet; but should some child of his be then living the poet would be believed.

It will be seen that the friend, being bid to give himself to another, offers his heart to the poet ; it is accepted, and thus ends the Introductory Argument.† The poet now fully accedes to his friend's desire, but only upon the strictest terms of marriage law. Since the poet is to be the means of preserving that beauty which he has so much advocated for another, he claims the same wedded rights for his Muse as that other would demand, to which the friend readily complies. Henceforth, till the verse

---

* Spenser, later in life, speaks of his then daring *apprentice quill.*

† The Muse, consequently, from this time hints of no other births than literary ones.

has attained its object, it is to record, jealously, watch-
fully, and lovingly, the faith and frailty of the object to
whom it is united, and to show a friendship which was
only to end in death.

Sonnet 18.—The theme of the poem is now commenced. To preserve the friend's youth and beauty, he
is married to immortal verse, which glories in the alliance.
The summer is now, in comparison with his friend's
eternal summer, all too changeful and brief; nor shall
death exult that his friend is hid in oblivious night, when
he becomes united to time with lines of ever-living verse,
and if he lives not in "children's eyes," he will in the
eyes of the world.

Sonnet 19.—The pregnant verse is already big with
the swelling argument. Time is defied, and told he
may now devour the earth's increase, but he is forbidden
the most heinous crime of carving a record of his
hours on the loved friend's brow. In despite of
time's wrongs his love shall appear in his verse ever
youthful.

As the first was a text Sonnet to those which followed
it, so also is the following, and from it spring those fantastic subtleties which have alone occasioned the mystery.
It will appear evident as we proceed that the young
friend made a voluntary promise that during the period
of the Sonnetting he would remain inviolate to the poet
and the Muse, and not seek the loving alliance of any
other, and the poet, on his part, determines to give up
himself and his Muse to the friend. Only from such a
promise could spring such fantastic writing. This would

bear resemblance to the whimsical decree, the occasion of so much sport, in " Love's Labour's Lost."

Sonnet 20.—A matchless description is now given of the loved friend who has thus eclipsed the customary mistress* by the marriage of verse, upon which Shakespeare, in the language of his own Posthumus, delighted to " rhyme upon 't, and vent it for a mockery." In a rhapsody the wedlock is consummated. The friend's effeminacy† is urged as a plea, and his attributes as an impulse to justify that which is written of him. The first line commences a satire upon mistress-sonnetting, and this satiric vein will be found to thread its way through the entire series. The rose of beauty in the friend's check is of Nature's own painting, not the result of art. The now ever youthful Master Herbert is styled the " master-mistress " of his passion, in the sense of the supreme object of his love, his best of friends, and more than mistress of his loving verse. Assuming man to be more constant than woman, he looks for an unbroken trothed friendship, and declares his eyes to be brighter than a woman's, and that he has become ennobled by their beaming upon him. In the climax of praise, the poet says he is "a man in hue, all hues in his controlling," *i. e.*, by his dual nature, the

---

* In that age the metamorphosis would not appear strange, it being then the common custom for boys and young men to take the female parts upon the stage.

† This praise was then thought the highest that could be offered to a youth. Bacon's eulogium upon Prince Henry is of a like tendency, and " Milton has the reputation of having been in his youth eminently beautiful, so as to have been called the lady of his college." (*Johnson's Lives*, p. 46.)

supreme beauty of the world and its chiefest ornament ;
and the poet conceives that Nature, as she wrought him,
designed at first making him a woman, but, falling in
love with her work, she made a man, forming a masterpiece by combining the excellences of the sexes ; so that,
like Nature, the poet makes a similar compound, making
him both his friend and mistress of his verse, and unwil-
lingly resolves to divide with women the love of his
friend. They are to treasure love's sweetest extraction ;
he will claim his intellectual love, his friendship.

Having described his dual nature as exceeding all
others, he in the next Sonnet qualifies that praise by
asserting that at least he is as beautiful as any other, and
that he himself is not, like others, writing false praise to
a false beauty. In accordance with this nature, and with
the youth being at once both the beloved of his Muse
and the mistress of his verse, through numerous Sonnets
the sex addressed is entirely concealed, while in other
Sonnets, for motives which will be shown, it is purposely
revealed ; and as the passion of the writer is also twofold,
being his own friendly love combined with the ardent
love of his Muse, so through numerous Sonnets their love
is united, thus forming the most loving mutual offering
of love to love ; and in other Sonnets the poet also
purposely divides his own love from his Muse's love,
the theme being both an alliance of friendship and
a marriage to the Muse.

Sonnet 21.—The poet enters upon his task pleased
with the idea that he is not following the customary
mode of mistress-sonnetting, as others were doing.

Catching up the theme of Sonnet 20, he declares that it was not a mere counterfeit beauty that incited his Muse to write, and as his rose was the rose of truth, he deserved all praise; and as it was the custom to over-praise, as if to sell, he, not desiring to part with his friend, will but speak the truth, which is that he is as fair as any mother's child (meaning of either sex), but that he is not so bright as the orbs of heaven.* Our poet would turn the accusation against himself had he not parody in view, which gives his pen free charter, both to imitate and excel. This Sonnet and the last should be considered as an assertion of both himself and his Muse being coupled to one of the highest worth, worthy of all praise.†

Sonnet 22 is begotten of this alliance; and the poet having in the 19th Sonnet declared that his love should appear ever youthful, it is now confirmed by his addressing him as such; and since the friends have exchanged hearts and become bosom friends, they are henceforth to be viewed as one. In spite of his glass he will consider himself as the reflection of his friend, and his friend's youth and beauty as his own. In this Sonnet the friend is urged to be regardful of himself for the poet's sake, as he will be of himself for the friend's, and should the friend ever desire to be severed from him, he cannot be, there can be no division between them, as by the wedding

---

* Spenser's "Amoretti" lays open to Shakespeare's charge, especially numbers 15, 26, 64, and 81; but as this is a shaft levelled at no poet in particular, and as Drayton was still writing, from what has been previously said, the allusion must be to him.

† One who deserved to be compared
  "With April's first-born flowers, and all things rare."

contract of verse they are made indivisible, the poet and
the friend are made one.

Sonnet 23.—Having now traced his plan, he likens
himself to one enacting some difficult part upon the
stage, who is either confused through fear or is unequal
to the task ; so he (feigning to mistrust his power) omits
to say the perfect ceremony of love's rite, in the presence
of his beloved (as an imperfect actor before his audience),
and seems bereft of the power of expressing his passion.
For this reason he entreats his friend to permit his book's
tongue to speak for him, so that during an absence which
will presently follow, the friend is desired, when reading
the Books of Sonnets the poet transmits him, which will
contain more love than he can express in his presence, to
suppose that his books are his looks, his pen his tongue,
and that, though absent, he hears him speak.   This the
fine sense of love will teach him.

It is evident from the tenour of the Sonnet, and
the expressions " forget to say " and " seem to decay,"
that the poet had ceased writing for a short time, and
that it is a plea for departure which may have engrossed
the poet's time at this juncture.   In Sonnet 117 he also,
after an interval of silence, speaks of his having forgotten
to write of his friend.

Sonnet 24.—He now informs his friend the result of
their loving union.   He has pictured upon his heart's
table his friend's image ; his friend has also drawn his.
Each has transferred the other's miniature reflection from
their eyes to their hearts.   He, however, laments that
eyes, though praised in the last Sonnet for their " fine

wit," have not, alas! cunning to discover the heart's constancy. Were it so, his friend would never misjudge
him, or he his friend.

Sonnet 25.—But the knowledge of their indissoluble
tie gladdens his heart; and as a reason for making his
intended journey the poet makes the first complaint at
his profession. He contrasts his position with that of
others, who are in favour with their stars. They may
boast of public honour and proud titles; but he has the
joyful consolation that, all unlooked for, these his covenant of friendship obtains him, though he will not (as the
next Sonnet informs us) partake of public honour through
his friend, advancing as a plea his own unworthiness. In
this spirit he exclaims:—Let the fickle favourites of
great princes boast of their honours; they exist but a
brief period in the sunshine of favour, they are soon
forgotten. How happy, then am I, that love and am
loved in return by one from whom I can neither remove
nor be removed.

The poet has now hinted his friend's princely greatness,
and has thus prepared the reader for the projected
journey, which, though it severs them, cannot remove
him from the breast of his friend, where he is constantly
fixed.

Sonnet 26.—The poet now bids him adieu, designating
him "lord of his love." He has already set out on the
meditated pilgrimage, and sends a written embassage of
seven Sonnets, not, he says, to show his wit, but to prove
that he is dutiful in absence, which absence he excuses,
thereby denoting that he is not worthy to remain before

his friend's eye ; and he requests his patron to adorn his
bare thoughts with some good conceits, till the star that
guides his moving shows him, by its gracious appearance,
to be worthy of his friend's respect. Till then he will
neither boast of his love nor be seen where his friend may
publicly acknowledge him.

The poet appears to be making his annual journey to
Stratford, and on this occasion is indeed the " Passionate
Pilgrim." He may have had private reasons of his own
for not notifying his destination, or he may have thought
it unworthy of notice. While away he wrote about forty
Sonnets. He is returned by the 67th. This separation
occurs, as will be seen, between the spring of 1599 and the
summer of 1601. It will also be seen that while absent
he probably visited Scotland for professional purposes.

Sonnet 27.—The poet, to show his untiring devotion
and constancy, and as witness that he at all times bears the
friend in memory, says that after a weary day's travel his
thoughts journey towards him, till in his sleep he beholds
his friend's spirit, which vision he occasionally addresses
during absence to beguile solitude. In this and the following Shakespeare imitates a Sonnet by Sidney to Stella, in
which day and night are confounded or made but one.

Sonnet 28.—He now demands how he can appear at
all presentable on his return,* each day adding to his
sorrows, and night nightly strengthening his grief, must
needs give him a woeful appearance, and prevents him
from fully adorning his love. Observe, the poet is as

---

* Thus excusing a premised poor show of love, and referring to their
separation and reunion (see Sonnet 26).

the clouded day, to which his friend is the sun giving glory.

Sonnet 29.—The complaint is now directed against fortune as the primary cause of their separation by debarring the poet from high titles, which want divides the friendship, and makes him both feel and appear an outcast, compelling him to live by public means, which brings disgrace upon him,* and makes him contented least with that which he enjoys most : he wishes for the art of one and the scope of another. He also desires youth beauty and friends, the while almost despising himself for these thoughts. Haply he thinks of his friend ! He is then joyful as the soaring lark, nor would he change his state with kings. Thus by his alliance, in friendship he has all his heart's desire, and partakes with his friend's love of all that his friend has and loves. The desiring this man's art and that man's scope was merely feigning, as in more advanced Sonnets he declares his patron was all his art, and that chanting his praise was all-sufficient scope.

Sonnet 30.—His sad solitude occasions a session of thoughts, wherein he summons up past things. He again complains of having wasted his time on a despised purpose. He laments the deaths of old departed friends and weeps afresh love's long since erased sorrows ; but, the remembrance of his living friend restores all losses, ends all griefs. The death of his son, mentioned in note to Sonnet 2, is probably the chief cause of this

---

* Davies observed in 1609, referring to Shakespeare, that though the stage stained pure gentle blood, yet he was a gentleman in mind and mood and the epithet "gentle" was applied to him by Jonson.

lament : he now looks upon Herbert as upon his own son
Hamnet. The opening and closing lines intimate that he
had long sought for a lordly constant lover for his Muse,
but now need seek no longer.

Sonnet 31.—His friend is the living altar of all those
friends he has loved and still loves. Thus he pictures to
himself for loving consolation how much he benefits by
friendship, how much it obtains him ; even so much
the friend receives from him ; he has all the love the
poet had given to past friends.

Sonnet 32.—Having spoken of the deaths of many
friends, he now reflects upon his own. He urges his
friend not to be sad if he should survive him, as he is
now, (having gained his utmost wish), prepared for death,
come when it will. His friend is told that though, after
his death, he may find better poets, he will not find such
another loving friend ; and in case the poet should not
live to adorn his tattered loving (the plea for absence in
the 26th), and the friend finds that other poets prove
better, he is desired to make this excuse for him :—Had
my friend's Muse grown with this growing age, he would
have brought forth a dearer birth than this, to march in
ranks better arrayed ; but since he died, and poets
prove better, I will read theirs for their style, his for his
love. The term growing age refers to the next age,
which another year (1599) would usher in. This missive
the following Sonnets prove, was now transmitted to
the friend.

The poet received an epistle in return to this embassage of seven Sonnets, in which he is told that

during absence his friend has already permitted a lady
to become the poet's rival, and receive loving favors,
supposed his alone, of whom the poet now lovingly
feigns to be jealous, as the friend had devoted his love to
the poet's Muse alone. Of this the poet forms two
groups of Sonnets, three in each group. Both the lady
and the friend in the first trio (Sonnets 33, 34, 35) are
blamed in the severest allegorical manner, but as they
both repent they are forgiven; and in the second trio
(Sonnets 40, 41, 42) the affair is lovingly turned to their
mutual advantage. The motive of the poet in pursuing
his loving calculations of loss and gain arises from the
conceit of the mutual gain of love their unity occasions,
and even this fancied loss proves an assured gain. In a
concluding Sonnet the poet blames himself for ever
having supposed such loss :—

> "Still losing, when I saw myself to win."

The poet acknowledges he loved the lady dearly before
the friend had an affection for her. He then argues that
she must love him, since she loves his dear friend, who is
himself. He goes still further, and poetically proves she
is his alone, because the two friends are one. Upon this
theme and its corollaries he expends ten Sonnets. Having
spoken in the last of the poorness of his verse, to disprove
the modest assertion he now puts forth all his power.

Sonnet 33.—This event is compared to the sun, which
often promises a fine day, but soon becomes disgraced by
treacherous clouds; so in the morning of their friendship
he is deprived of his friend's sunshine by a base cloud;
but as the sun of heaven is often thus disgraced, he will

not love his earthly sun the less for being so.   The lady, as
the severing cloud, is thus at once referred to with dis-
dainful reproaches.   This is continued in the next : she is
the envious cloud that either entirely robs the poet of the
friend's glory, or so much so that his influence is but partially felt.   The conceit of this and the following Sonnet is
imitated from the 40th and 46th of Spenser's " Amoretti."*

Sonnet 34.—He demands of the friend why, when he
promised such sunshine, he so suddenly allows another
to thus stand in his light, casting him in the shade.   It
is not enough that the friend asks forgiveness; the poet
bears the disgrace of the partial estrangement, it is he
who is the loser; but as the friend repents, that is
ransom sufficient.   Thus the poet went forth joyfully in
the sunshine of favour, confiding in the possession of the
friends love, but had he foreseen this event he would have
taken with him his cloak, *i.e.*, he would have prepared for
this tempest of tears.

Sonnet 35.—The friend has been likened to the sun
the lady is now spoken of as the moon ; they have both
proved guilty of the same faults, and are both in tears,
but there is no occasion for further grief.   All things and
all men have faults, even the poet, for authorising by
high compare this trespass on his right, palliating it with
the incense of verse, corrupts himself by becoming an
accessory to the lady to rob himself, so much he loves his
friend, and hates any other to possess him.   Thus the
friend is forgiven for the breach of faith to the poet's
Muse, purely because his love is stronger than his hate,

---

* In which Spenser pictures his, clouds of grief and storms of tears, when
leaving his beloved.

and the tears of the "sweet thief" (the lady) are rich pearls, a sufficient ransom for them both.

Sonnet 36.—Assuming that the friend by this breach desires to cancel the bond of loving fellowship, the poet admits for him that they must part. He supports his reason by contrasting the friend's position and power with his own despised state, and thus purposely compares his own compelled blots with his friend's voluntary stain. In the last it is intimated that the poet has become disgraced by gracing the friend's fault; now it is shown that it is the poet who will disgrace the patron, and will lovingly appear most in fault. Let me, he urges, confess that we must separate, although we are but one in love; so shall my blots be my disgrace alone. Though our loves are one our lives are unequally divided; and though this does not alter our love, yet it severs us. If his friend so desires it, he will never more claim his love, lest he should become shamed by the poet's lamented guilt; nor does he desire his friend to publicly honour him, fearing he should, by so doing, rob himself of his honour, as the poet considers him so much his better part that he would not thus bring shame upon him. The allusion to the spite of fortune is continued in the next, and he styles it " made lame." This telling epithet is used as an especial metaphor of defect as applied to himself. The player fears the peer, by the nearness of the tie, may partake of his disgrace, as he does of his friend's glories.

Sonnet 37.—Thus his love for his friend is as the love of an old doting father for his active child, whose deeds (see Sonnet 41, the friend's love for the lady is there said to be a deed of youth), he watches with delight. And the poet, being lamed by the direst spite of fortune, *i.e.*, separated from his friend by fortune's severest wrongs, being of mean estate and of despised profession, compared with the high position of his friend, receives all comfort from his goodness and constancy, for whatsoever crowning perfections he is blest with, with them the poet engrafts his love; so then, he is not lame, poor, nor despised (separated, of mean estate or despised profession), whilst this shadow* (his friend) gives such delight, that the poet is sufficed with his abundance; and whatever may be his crowning perfections, whether it be beauty, birth, wealth, or wit, be it all of these or any of these or more, he lives, partaking of the glory with his friend, in which he is supremely happy being thus, in spite of fortune, both present with his friend, and in the possession of youth, beauty, titles, and friends. By this covenant he partakes of his friend's glory and graces, as Jonathan did of David's.

Sonnet 38.—He now boasts that his Muse shall never want argument so long as his friend lives. Such expansion of theme is all sufficient, and too excellent for every common writer to indite. For this enlightenment, he avows that his friend is the tenth Muse—ten times worthier than the old nine others invocate; whoever writes of him is to give birth to eternal numbers, to outlive ages. At once humble, the poet adds: If my superficial Muse doth please these nice critical times, the praise

---

* Shadow is used in the same sense in the " Passionate Pilgrim :"—

" Wander a word for shadows like myself."

be thine,* I will labour. In this may be seen the desire that his friend in his absence will not accept the verses of an unworthy rival. The conceit of his being the tenth Muse is a quip at Drayton, having, in a Sonnet styled his mistress the "ninth worthy," making, as Sir J. Davies said in an Epigram, "his mistress march with men of war," and he levels a shaft also at the unworthy uses the old Muses had been brought to, they were so degraded he would invoke none of them. It appears also that Shakespeare's friends had intimated to him that his verses were already in request among the "private friends ;" and it is denoted that the Sonnets were evidently to be viewed as Herbert's, as Sidney's "Arcadia" was to be known as the "Countess of Pembroke's Arcadia." The allusion may also be to the praise given by Meres in his "Wits Treasury" of 1598, when writing of the Muses speaking English in Shakespeare's "fine filed phrase," and of these "sugar'd Sonnets," as witness of his excellence. Thus, the poet's Muse, by reason of her wedlock, transfers herself and her literary births to the friend, who may, on this account, be said to be the tenth Muse.

Sonnet 39.—Having declared the honour to be his friend's alone, he finds occasion to again excuse the absence. They being but one, the praise is also his own, which it would be an impropriety to sing were he not absent. It also alleviates the pangs of absence to write thus, and instructs the poet how to make distance near at hand, and but one a division, by praising the friend as present with him though absent.

---

* Or, as T. Heywood says, "these more exquisite and refined times."—*Prologue to The Four Apprentices*, 1615.

By the conceit of their oneness, the praises bestowed
upon his friend would be but sinful self-praise, then it
were better they were divided, not only by distance, but
in personality. The following three Sonnets embrace this
distinction, though they end attesting their unity.

Sonnet 40.—The subject suspended in Sonnet 35 is
resumed in this and in the two following, in which a
computation is made, showing that, by their unity and
triplicity, the loves of either belong to but one ; and that
the friend's lady love, whom the poet had previously
loved, by her loving his friend, now not only loves him
also, but is alone the poet's, so that from fearing to be a
loser, he rejoices to find himself a gainer. Thus, in this
Sonnet, he bids his friend, whom he views as the image
and personification of all love, to take all his loves* which
he has hitherto received. The friend is not blamed for
accepting the lady's love (it is thus intimated that had
Shakespeare chosen a mistress for his friend, this is the
lady he would have selected), but he is to blame himself for
partaking of woman's love after his repeated refusals (see
Sonnets 10 and 16), and for giving his love to another,
after vowing it the poet's alone, thus causing a threefold
theft—robbing the poet of his all in all, *i.e.*, of himself, the
friend, and the lady. But this must not occasion a separation of friendship, since it is better to bear a loving
wrong than an injurious hate, so the wantonness in his
friend appears all for the best.

Sonnet 41.—The fault is again confessed to be but a

---

* "Take all my loves," *i.e.*, friendly loves, as in 30 and 31. Their mutual
loving, divested of allegory, was but pure friendship, as will be seen between
both the poet, the friend, and the mistress.

petty wrong. The young friend is excused for being led away at the time his heart forgets its friendly tie, and is assailed by woman's love. It was too much to assume he could withstand it. What youth would sourly disdain the sweet love of a woman, or leave her till she is won. Ah me! the poet sighs, my dearest love you should have foreborne, and have blamed thy youth and beauty which compel thee to sever a twofold troth. By giving his love to the lady and receiving hers, he robs the poet of his own love and hers also ; the poet, though not her real lover, had possessed her loving friendship (see Sonnet 136, but in the following Sonnet the theme ends in sweet mutual concord).

Sonnet 42.—The poet now consoles himself with the thought that his vision of the unity was but disturbed by a passing cloud. It is not the friend possessing the lady which grieves him, though it may be said he loved her dearly before she stole his friend ; but how could he love the " sweet thief" that had thus taken his coveted jewel? The loving offenders are, however, thus excused : It is assumed that the friend loves her because he knows the poet loves her, and even so she loves the friend because she knows the poet loves him, so that the love is of mutual approval, and by the sweet delusive flattery that the poet and the friend are one, he concludes that she alone loves him.*

The Epistle of the friend thus answered, he returns to his former topics,† and flatters himself as still holding loving possession, though but in a dream.

---

* In the " Two Gentlemen of Verona," act ii., sec. 6, there is a similar romantic mystification of love and friendship.

† From hence throughout the Epistles to the friend no further direct allusion is made to the mistress, the poet would not destroy the illusion.

Sonnet 43.—Having discoursed of his jealousy, he anew details his loving thoughts during absence. His mental sight in deepest sleep sees clearer than his eyes in open day. The friend's bright shadow is seen in dreams in the dead night, but it would occasion more joy to see his actual substance in the living day, for absence confounds the day and night, or makes them as but one.

Sonnet 44.—As if still addressing his friend's spirit, he exclaims: Could I move my self as quick as thought, I would at once conquer the distance between us, but I must wait in sadness time's leisure, overcome with tears. The love still strengthens, and the friend might have exclaimed with the Psalmist David, " Thy love to me was wonderful, passing the love of woman" The eyes of the Muse shed heavy tears, fearing she may yet lose her beloved, whom she has more than won. The last lines allude to, and are in contrast to the lovers in tears (see Sonnet 35).

Sonnet 45.—Having discoursed of the two grosser elements of the four which were then the theory of life, of the two more ethereal, he continues : Thin air and purifying fire are with thee wherever I abide—the first, his thought, the other, his desire, are ever present-absent, ever going and returning in tender embassies of love, causing alternate joy and sorrow. In this, allusion is made to the embassies of love which have just passed between them.

Sonnet 46.—Addressing the mental vision, he says further : Mine eye and heart contend for the conquest of thine image, each asserts the right to claim thy possession, upon which my thoughts holding session, decide that the lucid eye may claim thy outward appearance, and the loving heart thy inward love of heart.

Sonnet 47.—They are now on terms of amity, they love one object and each other, and are both delighted with the counterfeit vision, awake or sleeping. Thus, by bearing his friend's form constantly in his eye and love in his heart, they are still together, in spite of the separation. The poet dwells on his theme like an air in an opera constantly recurring with variations.

Sonnet 48.—Before setting out on his journey, the poet placed under lock and key those things which he desired to find for himself on his return; but his friend, to whom his jewels were but trifles, was left a prey to every vulgar thief, alluding to the rhymers pointed out in Sonnet 38, as seeking patronage. The friend is kept close in no chest save the poet's bosom, and even from thence he fears he may be stolen, for the virtuous prove thievish for precious treasures, indirectly alluding to his rival, the youth's lady love. The leading characteristic of these poems is jealousy, and it being an attribute of the highest love, it is given to his Muse. The third line of this Sonnet is explained by the third line of the 78th: the poet desired that upon his return his friend should be reserved for his own pen alone.

Sonnet 49.—In case the time should ever come when the friend should steal or be stolen from him, when his friend may frown on his unworthiness, induced to do so by self-respect and graver years, against that time the poet the poet stands armed with his pen against himself; and in his verse, with self-knowledge of his own desert, he will raise his hand against himself, to guard his friend's lawful reasons, for the friend has every right to leave him, since, why the poet should claim his love he will assert no cause, so that, should the patron ever desire to end the friendship, the poet will justify his conduct.

Sonnet 50.—Such thoughts, while journeying from his friend cannot but weigh heavily upon him, insomuch, that the horse which bears him feels the weight of sorrow, and plods heavily on, as if by some instinct he knew that his rider loved not haste when journeying from his friend. Though he was journeying to Stratford, the poet might well exclaim, " My grief lies onward, and my joy behind," for in this allegorical parody all family love is purposely avoided. As before hinted, he may now be journeying to Scotland. This and the following are imitated from Sidney's 49th Sonnet to Stella.

Sonnet 51.—The ever excusing poet now makes a plea for the horse. The sagacious animal knows there is no need of posting till he returns ; its dull heavy composition cannot kept pace with winged desires. But while his steed plods on at a slow pace, his thoughts run swiftly towards his friend, so that in going he is ever returning with the celerity of thought. This and following Sonnet are but variations of the 44th and 45th.

Sonnet 52.—He is now consoled with the idea that there is real benefit in this separation, since that which he covets does not become common by being daily seen. He has lamented (Sonnet 48) that he had not locked up his chief jewel, his friend, before leaving ; but time has secured him as in a chest, the key of which is some "blessed instant" which will newly unfold his "imprisoned pride." Blessed then is he whose possession is a triumph, and whose loss is such hope of reunion. Their meetings coming but seldom, like the yearly festivals, will afford the more delight.

In the next Sonnet the poet again invokes the spirit of his absent friend, and relates the supremacy of his beauty and the infinite bounty of his love, together with his matchless constancy, and though he seldom sees or hears from him, he fully confides in his love.

Sonnet 53.—The apparently double nature, the theme of the 20th Sonnet, is again renewed. He demands of his friend, how comes it that his form holds supremacy over all visible objects. His beauty exceeds that of Adonis or of Helen ; he is the beauty of the spring and the bounty of the harvest, all visible things partake of his blessed shape ; but for constancy of heart he is himself alone, for though he had proved, to the poet's advantage, allegorically faithless to the Muse, he was literally faithful to the poet ; and weighing the affection of his friend with his own, it is assumed that he will ever remain true. We have seen in Sonnet 37, in what manner Shakespeare partook of his bounty. The sixth couplet of the Sonnet again takes up the satire. The Muse bids the object of her love, set, that is, add to, the beauty of womanly beauty ; and he is but rearrayed in Grecian dressings, or in other words, his beauty is but imitated, for what has been said of ancient beauty is his praise.

Sonnet 54.—As this praise would be excessive if not addressed to true beauty and goodness, the truth and virtue of beauty's rose is now extolled. Though others, "painted beauties" (Sonnet 21), may bear as deep a flush as his friend's natural tint, which is compared to a sweet garden rose, in contrast to the common hedge roses of others, which bear no smell or lasting sweetness, while of the garden roses are made the sweet odours, so when his outward beauty fades, his inward virtue shall be distilled by the chemistry of verse. This has reference to Sonnets 5 and 6 ; by virtue of verse, that which the friend refrained from doing is accomplished, and it also attests that with external graces, he possesses inward goodness and sweetness.

Sonnet 55.—Pursuing the subtle allusions to Sonnets 5 and 6, and to the eleventh line of the first, the " Proud Sonnet," has become the phial which shall preserve his sweet contents ; and containing such treasure has become big with conception, and is conscious of its power to preserve his outward beauty and inner virtue eternally ; in it his friend shall stand before the eyes of the world an ever living monument, when princes' tombs and places of strength are annihilated, he shall go onward. Thus, till he arrives at the judgment, he lives in verse and dwells in the eyes of lovers, since the verse, as in the following, is full of love.

The poet in this Sonnet mocks the vaunts of the inflated sonnetting of the day—for particular examples see Spenser, Sonnets 69, 75, 82; Daniels, 41, 42, 52 ; Drayton, 6, 44, 47. It is remarkable that no sonnetting of such bombastic nature appeared after these of Shakespeare's.

Sonnet 56.—After this triumphant flourish the poet addresses his love, and desires it to sustain its power, to

have daily appetite, be daily fed, and not sicken and die
to still beguile the tediousness of absence by dwelling on
his friend's image both by day and night; "The spirit of
love" is to permit this sad interim to be like the ocean
which parts the shore, where two newly contracted daily
come, that when they see return of love more blest may be
the view; or call it weary winter, their meeting will be a
desired summer. This refers to Sonnet 44, which describes the friend as visiting him in a vision and returning. Being two newly contracted, they cannot but ever
have each other in memory, and desire a real meeting.

In the two following, the poet declares, in witness of
his entire submissiveness, that all his thoughts and affairs
are entirely subservient to his friend's will.

Sonnet 57.—Directly addressing the Spirit of Love* as
his sovereign lord, he will wait in uncomplaining sadness
for the time he may desire thus to visit him; nor will he
question with jealous thought his friend's affairs, save that
where he is he makes others happy. So foolish is the
poet's love, that whatever his friend may do, he will
submit to his will in all loving servitude, and find no
fault. The poet appears to refer to the lady, knowing that
many have lost dear friends by such alliances; either
dividing the affection or engrossing it altogether. Such
a one is indeed a rival. In this and the following, the
poet blames himself for having presumed to accuse his
friend of injuring him, or demanding how he spent his
time, when he is at liberty to do what he chooses when-

---

* Compare the 8th line of this Sonnet with the 10th line of the 44th, for
such address and allusion.

ever he may desire, so forgiving and loving is the poet's
Muse.

Sonnet 58.—The God of Love which made him first
his friend's slave (of love) forbade that he should even in
thought control his pleasure, or that his friend should be
demanded how he spent his time, as the poet is but his
friend's vassal, awaiting his bidding, (see Sonnet 26), and
sovereign power* giving him the right not only to make
a breach of friendship, but pardon himself for the fault.
Meanwhile the poet will calmly wait, and suffer the pangs
of absence without complaint. He has shown that the
separation is for his friend's advantage, and desires that
he will still permit him to remain in solitude, while he
may mingle with others as he chooses. The 6th line of
this Sonnet refers to the 12th of the 52nd Sonnet. Time
is the jailer, and when he wills it, and his friend bids him,
they will meet. It is also hinted that the patron needs
not the poet's pardon for this crime, as he has the power
to pardon himself, so no more will be said of it. This
Sonnet evidently refers to Sonnets 41 and 144.

Sonnet 59.—Having declared him to be his sovereign,
he now contrasts him with the subjects of other poet's
verses ; as if for a plea for his singular writing, he desires
to see. As he tells the friend, if that which is hath been
before, what the ancients would have said in the world,
" to this composed wonder of your frame," whether we
excel them, or they us in beauty. Oh! I am sure, he
concludes, the learned of a former age, to less worthy

---

* The 87th hath also a similar reference.

subjects gave lofty praise. The third *couplet* points to the assumed duality of his nature, as denoted in Sonnets 20 and 53.

Sonnet 60.—After looking backward into times long past, he now glances at the future. He is prophetic as to his verse in better new times; and though still at a distance from his friend, the lines seem to denote that he was contemplating retracing his way, like the waves towards the shore. This conjecture is supported by sequent Sonnets. He continues the apostrophe to the youth of beauty, exclaiming: That birth, from the night of oblivion to the light of day, advances to maturity, wherewith being crowned, his glory becomes obscured by the shadows of age, and Time that gave, now destroys the gift. All things are cut down by his scythe, but the poet's verse shall stand in spite of him. Thus, though all things are changed, the verse shall remain unchanged, implying that a literary birth far exceeded a natural one in outliving ages.

Sonnet 61.—Assured of the future constancy of his verse, he now discovers his own fixed devotedness, by which he is rendered a slave to love, dejected and weary of having one thought, and one object continually before him, and he demands of his friend whether it is by his will his spirit wanders so far, standing ever as a watchman over him. Is he as jealous of the poet, as the poet is of him? O! no, the poet says, it is my love for thee that keeps me watching while thou art afar off, with others all too near, alluding to the love the friend had for the lady, and to her having placed his love in her heart. This Sonnet is in contrast to the 57th and 58th. There the

G

poet speaks of his having discovered the friend to be
guilty ; the friend's spirit is now supposed to be jealously
watching over the poet to discover inconstancy in him,
or waste of time.

Sonnet 62.—He is, however, consoled in these medita-
tions, as in Sonnets 22 and 39, with the thought that
though separated he is still with him.   The praise is then
his own, and this sweet flattery fills him with self-love, for
which iniquity he upbraids himself ; his glass enforces the
truth ; he sees himself in it, in intellectual vision, not in the
fresh morning of budding youth, but as antiquity stamped
and stained with years.   'Tis thee, myself, he says, for
whom I praise myself, adorning my defeatured age with
thy youthful beauty.

From this time the vision of the friend as the spirit of
love is no more addressed ; and in the following six Sonnets, the poet soliloquises his thoughts.   This upbraiding
of his own self-love, as sequent Sonnets will prove, is but
an excuse for silence on his journey back, and for speedy
conclusion to the song on his return.   The reader will
discover that in the next and two following Sonnets,
the poet still personates antiquity, and contrasts Times
pilgrimage with his own.   This is confirmed by Sonnet
64.   He depicts himself as of ancient visage, both as
a foil to set off the beauty of his friend, and as testimony of his excelling worth.   This is done in imitation
of the sonnetteers who call Time to witness the perfections of their mistresses.   It also shows more vividly
Time's ravage of beauty, and is a plea for the poet's
striving to keep him ever youthful in his verse.   It is
evident from what follows, that the series of Sonnets,

from the 42nd to the 65th, end the Sonnets written in absence, and it may be assumed were sent to the friend from the extreme end of his journey.

Sonnet 63.—The aged portrait* the poet has drawn of himself, the wrinkled face of grave antiquity, is still further touched upon; and this preparation of verse is made against the time when his loved friend's morn shall have journeyed on to the dark precipice of age, and his beauties have become obscured; and though Time cuts from memory the lover's life, the poet's lines shall preserve his beauty in all its freshness.

Sonnet 64.—The thoughts of his death recall to his ancient memory, from what he has seen, that he can but lead a brief life, since antiquity has witnessed, defaced by Time's fell hand, the proud, costly erections of a long past age; once lofty towers, overthrown and obliterated, and eternal brass succumb to man's destruction. When he has seen the devouring ocean and the firm land change places,† or state itself utterly annihilated, ruin bids him remember that Time will come and take away the object of his love. The thought is as a death; he cannot but weep to possess that which he fears to lose. Thus antiquity (in the person of the poet) bears witness that the friend is most worthy of being loved, and fears to lose by death one so beautiful.

Sonnet 65.—The complaint is renewed. Amidst such

---

* A parallel view is here taken of the lines of age and of verse; the former, as Montaigne would say, " Were wrinkles imprinted on the mind, not in the face."

† He now speaks of the loss and gain Time has witnessed as contrast to his own loss and gain in love.

universal annihilation, what can become of beauty, whose
strength is but as a flower, which cannot withstand Time's
decay! Who can preserve it? What strong hand can
withhold Time's progress, or forbid his spoil of beauty?
None; unless black ink has the miraculous power of
keeping it brightly shining in darkness.* Compare this
with the 12th, where Shakespeare would give no hope of
this being effected but by children; resigned to his friend's
desire verse is now to attain this object. The poet then
expressed his own wish, he now fulfils the will of his
friend and the desire of his Muse.

The poet has now returned. This was between the
years 1600 and 1601, as will be presently shown. It is
strange that there is no mention made of the anticipated
joyful meeting at this juncture. There were probably
circumstances which Shakespeare did not choose to
insert in this poetical diary, as it may have been a
felicity which he chose the reader to imagine rather
than himself describe. That their reunion was the cause
of mutual joyfulness, will be evident, if it is not observed in
the following twelve Sonnets, for they, with those from
the 60th (which were written when the poet was contemplating a speedy return) form the most profound and beautiful group of the whole series, and end the first poem.

Sonnet 66.—The poet now speaks in his own person
The war against Time has ceased; the times are now
attacked. Upon the abuses which he observes on his return, he exclaims,—Weary with all these, I desire the

---

* In contrast to SS. 43 and 61, that the verse may be like the black
night filled with the bright vision of the friend.

peaceful rest death affords. Beholding the worthy but poorly born and of mean estate, the most abject gaily arrayed, and in the best of faith, the most lamentable perjury; the highest honour wrongfully given, and the virtuous maiden proclaimed a strumpet; perfection itself vilely disgraced, and strength being withheld made powerless; art* silenced by authority, and folly (the professor) mastering ability (the unskilled); plain truth, miscalled folly, and goodness, a captive, serving captain ill; weary with these, from these I would depart, save that by dying I am severed from my loved friend. This lament is occasioned by the poet's watchful regard for his patron, amid the evils with which he was surrounded; of which the poet himself is weary, and would desire death were it not for his friend's sake, since there is nothing in the world for which he cares except his friend's love. The vile times thus proved unworthy of both the poet and the patron; and the poet speaking in the name of his muse, would, were it not for the sake of her beloved, at once end her poetic life. In the two following Sonnets the friend's face is said to be as a map of the beauty of antiquity, these Sonnets the poet purposely made in contrast to the picture of himself as antiquity.

Sonnet 67.—He sighs to find his friend has to live amid such depravity. The times being so corrupt, he fears his friend may be blamed with them; hence several Sonnets harp upon this chord. Ah! (the poet sighs) wherefore should he (the love of the last line of the previous Sonnet) live amidst the world's contagion,

---

* Dramatic art.

gracing profanity with his presence, in such impious
times of profaned beauty? Why should poor beauty
steal lifeless imitation of his living hue? Why should
she deceitfully seek painted roses, since his is the true
one? Why should he live, now nature is so impo-
verished of rosy blushes?—possessing no riches but his;
and proud of many, centres her reputation upon one. Him
she richly values, as showing her wealth in ancient times,
before these last, so degenerate. This is a variation of the
first lines of the commencing Sonnet of this series (21) :—

> " So it is not with me as with that Muse,
> Stirred by a painted beauty to his verse."

Nothing seems to have met Shakespeare's reproach so
much as face-painting. To make his own case good
he continues in the satiric vein.* The theme of the
poet's Muse being, Why should my lovely truthful rose
become disgraced by living with the false? of whom Nature
is ashamed. The poet might have added, in his own words,
from "Troilus and Cressida :—" Had I a sister were a
grace, or a daughter a goddess, he should take his choice."

Sonnet 68—Therefore his friend's cheek is the map
of days quite gone, when beauty lived and died as
flowers do now; before the illegitimate signs of beauty
were displayed, or dared find residence on a living
head; before the valued tresses of the dead (the right of
sepulchres) were shorn away to live again upon the head
of another; before buried beauty's fleece appeared upon a

---

* Stubbs in his "Anatomy of Abuses," 1585, warns the fair sex against
incurring the displeasure of heaven for these offences; and Ophelia has
the ironical term "beautified" applied to her by her satirical lover,
Hamlet. Nevertheless, allowing for change of time and customs, the poet's
argument still stands good—witness rouge and chignons, the technical term
for hair from the tomb is " Churchyard hair."

second head. In him are seen those ancient sacred hours without adornment; beautiful in himself, not the reaped growth of another summer. Robbing from none of the past to give him present beauty, he is stored by nature as a map, to show adulterous art what beauty was formerly. Thus these times of sinful infectious impiety are contrasted with his holy antique hours of living truth, and the question is answered, "Wherefore with infection should he live?" and the Muse has affirmed that without false ornament her beloved was the most beautiful. The drift of the Muse is that a mere mortal woman is not worthy of him; she is indirectly warring with her rival. The last Sonnet being mainly upon painting the face, this upon dressing the head.*

Sonnet 69.—Having spoken of the corruptions of the times—amongst other things of right perfection being wrongfully disgraced—his friend is now adduced as an example of the world's misjudgment, and vindicated, though at the same time warned. He is told:—Those of thy parts which are viewed by the eye of the world want nothing that the innermost thoughts of the world can better: the tongues of all souls proclaim this thy due, which is the plain truth. They allow the sovereignty of thy outer graces, but of thy beauty of mind they guess by what they see of thy actions; then wilfully, although their eyes were loving, they add to thy beautiful flower the rank smell of weeds. But wherefore does not thy odour match thy appearance? The solution is this:— Thou art becoming common! The poet has complained

---

* It must be remembered this was written during the last years of Elizabeth, when these arts were in the height of fashion.

in the 61st of his being all too near with others while
absent from him.

Sonnet 70.—Ceasing to warn him further, he boldly
rebuts the slander, and turns it to the friends advantage.
Though thou art blamed, the poet continues, it shall not be
to thy dishonour; for slander (a crow that flies in the
sweetest air of heaven) ever levels at the beautiful. While
you remain virtuous, slander, which in these ill times is
courted, but attests your innocence, as canker vice loves
the sweetest buds. Thou presentest a pure spotless manhood ;* thou hastpassed by the dangers of youth either un-
unassailed by slander, or victorious, being so. Though
thou deservest this praise it has not the power to silence
envious detractors ; they are never tongue-tied, and were it
not for slander and envy you would be universally beloved. He thus attests the truth of his beauty and
virtue :—He is far too good to live in times so bad ; his
only fault is that by associating too much with the world
he has become blamed with the blameworthy. Hence the
deep sigh commencing Sonnet 67. We shall show in more
advanced Sonnets the occasion which especially gave rise
to this slander, rebuke, and warning.

Having brought the poem to an intended conclusion,
the poet gives his loved friend some instructions how to
act in the event of his own death, desiring him to deny
the friendship, lest it bring him disgrace.

Sonnet 71.—As if to console his friend, the poet

---

* The poet may well say this of his friend, the past offence (S.s. 33 to
43) being, as shown, merely allegorical. In this instance it is a real fault,
though not meriting the censure of either the world or the poet. Ben
Jonson also extols him as an example of virtue in an age of vice (see
Additional Notes to this Sonnet).

pictures the usage he has received from "the wise world."
Returning to the theme of separation by death (and
these sad thoughts well nigh occasion such a desire), and
perhaps as a testimony to the purity of his ardent friendship, especially as since his return he has written still
more solemnly and sadly, he cries out, in the bitterest
strain :—Mourn no more for me when I am dead than
the time you hear the surly sullen bell toll forth to the
world that I am gone from this vile world to dwell with
vilest worms ; and if you read this line, remember not
the hand that wrote it ; for my love for you is such that
I would be forgotten if you should be saddened by
remembrance of me. If you should look upon this verse
when I am mingled with clay, do not so much as utter
my name, but let your love die with my life, lest the
" wise world " should observe your sorrow, and deride you
with me after I am dead. The " wise world," which had
judged the friend wrongfully, was equally unjust to the
poet's merits. The poem coming to an end, that it may contain a complete testimony of love, the poet speaks of death
and the grave, which will alone separate and end their love.

Sonnet 72 harps ironically upon the same mournful
note. Lest (says the poet) you should be tasked to
recount what merit I possessed when living that you
should esteem after my death, dear love, forget me quite ;
for you can tell of nothing worthy in me, unless you
devise something false beyond my desert, and honour me
with more praise when dead than careful truth would freely
offer. Lest you should then be accused of a lie out of
love for me, bury my name with my body, that it may no

longer live for thy or my shame ; for I am disgraced by
that which I give birth to, so are you to love things unworthy.   The poet fears his Sonnets will be condemned
because their author has appeared upon the public stage.

Sonnet 73.—Having given reasons which the world
held sufficient for his friend to dislike him, he now
instances one why he should love him.   Reproducing the
picture of himself advanced in years, in proof of his
love only ending with his life, the bright morning of his
friend's youth is again contrasted with the shadows of
age in which the poet is enshrouded, as a foil to their
mutual glory.   In this strain, but in a more cheerful
tone, he continues thus :—Thou mayst in me behold
(intellectually) that season of the year when few or no
yellow leaves hang upon the bare choirs of the weather-
beaten boughs, where the sweet birds were wont to sing.
I appear to thee as the twilight of a day in autumn, when
in the west the setting sun fadeth, which soon black
night, the shadow of death, taketh away.   It is this that
impels thee to love that which thou must soon lose.
Thus, though crumbling in the ashes of age, he dwells
for ever in the presence of immortal youth.   The poet
assumes the cessation of the Sonnets to be the end of his
poetic life, to which he makes allusion in the words,
" Where late the sweet birds sang," the end of the
poem being figuratively the end of his own life.   His
friend may love him, not for his merit, but because he
will look upon him as an old friend, from whom he must
soon part ; so that instead of Shakespeare meditating,
as has been hitherto supposed, an early death, he was

looking to live to a good old age, as figured by him in the Sonnet, that his love and verse might bear witness together.

Sonnet 74.—As death may separate them, he requests his friend to be prepared, without complaint, for the time when the fell sergeant Death, without all bail, shall carry him away, as he will still live in the memorial of friendship which is his better part. The earth will have his earth, his baser substance. His lifeless body, the mere prey of worms, is unworthy of his friend's remembrance, being the coward conquest of Time's vile knife; it is not his baser part, but his better part, which it is his will should remain with his friend. So Henry V. speaks of his baser part as " this frail and worthless trunk." The poet still descants upon the saddest of themes, as if he felt that tombs wanted tongues; and when we gaze upon the Stratford monument we can but rejoice to know that we may still hear the poet speak in these poems which he loved so much, and in which he has bequeathed to us his innermost thoughts.

Having meditated upon death, he now speaks of that from which he receives present life, which he may well do, as the friend does not with the world despise him.

Sonnet 75.—His friend is as the very life of his thoughts, or as the gentle showers of the seasons are to the earth. Thus his friend occasions in him the flowers of fancy to spring forth; and for his possession he holds such strife as a miser for his wealth; now proud of having him, and then fearing the filching age will steal his treasure; now counting it better to enjoy his friendship in absence, then thinking it better that the world may see his pleasure;

sometimes overjoyed at his society, at another time quite bereft of it, having or striving for no delight but what his friend affords. Thus the poet from time to time is either bereft of him altogether, or enjoying his society to abundance. This must also be considered as a reason for ceasing the song, since for the muse to surfeit to such excess in his presence, is worse than to pine in absence—see Sonnets 39, 52, 118, 119. This Sonnet indicates that since the poet's return, they were much in each others company.

Sonnet 76.—With an unalterable love, why should the song alter, assuming that the monotonous strain it still takes may be supposed a fault. It had become customary to change both the subject and style of the verse, but as the poet writes still to one and of one, his verse, like himself, is ever the same, being the servant of one master, it ever appears in the same dress. Hence, his verse is a type of his constancy, and every word denotes its author and his love.

Sonnet 77.—It is further shown that there is no need of varying the theme, or even of continuing it. Fearing, as a further Sonnet indicates, to make himself too common, as so many birds of a like feather were then in wild song and ready to chant his patron's praise, he thought it were wise to cease, which he accordingly did, and bids him a present farewell. The plea for so doing is that the task the poet set himself is now accomplished, namely, the making a lasting record of his patron's youth, beauty, and friendship. Hence the poet's verse need not tell him the marks made by Time's progress, his glass will do that, and every wrinkle remind him of an open grave ; nor need it upbraid him with the waste of time, the clock will do that. With this

L'Envoy is also presented a book for the purposes of study,
From Sonnet 23, it has been already seen that Shakespeare
promised Books of Sonnets to his friend. This promise,
as will be seen, was not fulfilled to the friend's satisfaction.
To the present book there were leaves remaining blank,
upon which the friend was told to nurse the offspring
begotten by his own fancy, both for his own advantage
and his book's enrichment. This was a high compliment,
and it is pleasant to observe that the vices of frailty
in friendship, so strongly depicted in these verses of
Shakespeare, were afterwards also censured by Lord
Herbert himself in his own poems. Thus ends the first
division, which divides the poem into two parts. The
somewhat abrupt ending of the song may have been
occasioned by the death of Lord Herbert's father in the
autumn of 1601, and by the death of the poet's father,
which occurred a little later in the same year.

The length of the interim between the cessation and
renewal of the chain of Sonnets, may be gathered from the
following circumstances to have been about twelve months
duration. Between 1601-2, the company of players to
which Shakespeare belonged returned from the Scotch
Court, with a bounty of £400 for their services. They had
been absent from Oct. 1599 to Dec. 1601, and it appears that
a few months after this date Shakespeare ceased writing.
For further particulars concerning the visit of Shakespeare's company to Scotland consult Knight and Collier's
editions of Shakespeare. Mr. Collier informs us that the
poet's absence from Stratford was longer than usual
during this period, and that probably he visited the
Scotch capital, and these poems indicate that at this date
he made a lengthened journey.

The occasion which stirred our poet to readdress his friend, arose from rival poets dedicating works to his coveted friend; this was in 1603, and fixes the date early in that year. Upon the entry of James to take possession of the throne of England, the king stayed at Wilton (the ancestral home of the Earls of Pembroke), during his progress through his new kingdom, upon which occasion Shakespeare's company of players was invited by the young Earl to entertain the king; and there is probability that it was at the injunction of James that Macbeth was written. To this occasion also the player-editors of the first folio may refer when speaking of Shakespeare having been so highly favoured by the Earls of Pembroke, of which they bore witness. Tradition affirms that James wrote a letter to Shakespeare, and received some verses in return. Thus we determine that the song ceased between 1601 and 1602, and began again in 1603.*

Sonnet 78.—As if because of the poet's ceasing the song, the patron-friend affects to favour other poets. Shakespeare commences by reminding the young lord that he was his first poet, and that others, who had no claim on him, were imitating his example, and were making that use of him which was his own privileged right His friend's eyes, which he extolled in the first Sonnet, he again praises; they not only attracted Shakespeare, but now incite others; and by looking favourably upon him and his writing they had raised him from earth to heaven. The patron-friend must be most proud of that which Shakespeare compiles, as he is the only begetter,

---

* The renewal of our poet's sonnetting appears to have began early in 1603, and lasted till midsummer of the same year, so that upon the visit of James the friend would possess the entire series.

and the poems are begotten by his inspiration alone on the
the poet's brain, he being married to his Muse; in others,
he is but partially felt, and but adds grace to graces, while
he is all the poet's art, and his verse is exalted by writing
of his friend's excellences. Thus, as in Sonnet 38 the
patron is to receive all praise; without him the poet
esteems himself nothing. In the first series, he denotes
that he derived his knowledge from his friend's eyes; he
now asserts they are alone his intellectual light. The poet
is careful in renewing the song to attach it to the former
part, the tenth line of this being linked to the eleventh
line of the last Sonnet.

Sonnet 79.—Another now partakes of his friend's
grace, and to him Shakespeare is willing to resign office.
Our poet's gracious numbers having come to an end, the
result is that a worthier pen (the patron's desert) is used,
which is to bring forth a better conception. But what
Shakespeare's rival offers is but stolen. He gives virtue
and beauty : the one he stole from the patron's course of
life, the other from his cheek; nor can he offer any praise
that does not already live in him. The patron is, then,
to thank him not for what he lends, since the debt the
rival owes the patron himself pays. It will presently be
shown that the rival still owed a promised debt, but now
is come too late to pay it. This Sonnet and two others
which follow bear testimony to the statement made in
the 77th, that there is now no occasion for Shakespeare,
much less another, to celebrate his patron's praise; for
the friend is himself his own living praise, and when he
dies the Sonnets will keep it ever living. Our poet
feigns that his Muse fell sick and became silenced by
seeing such mighty rivals arising.

Who this rival was who with others sought the young earl's patronage has been already mentioned in the Preliminary Remarks; and in the Notes appended to this Essay evidence is adduced to establish beyond a doubt that it is he to whom Shakespeare chiefly alludes; and were it not by being, as Davies himself admits, graced by eternal lines, he would be permitted to fall silently into oblivion. The manner in which he is satirised is worthy attention, and the reader will not fail to perceive the ironical touches the friend receives for giving him countenance. The allusions to the other poets are given in the Additional Notes.

Sonnet 80 is imbued with the spirit of satire; hence the poet feigns to fear competition with his rival, whose verse is compared to a vessel of " tall building and goodly pride," afloat in the flood of prosperity, in comparison to which the verse of Shakespeare is an impudent petty bark. The poet further adds :—Then if he gain thy love, and I am cast off, my worst fault is that my love is alone the cause, since (as he concludes the 32nd Sonnet) I write, not to show my wit, but my love. He thus changes situation with his antagonist, the description of his own verse being but a just description of that of his rival.

Sonnet 81 refers to the fear expressed in the last that his sick love may decay and die. This leads him to meditate upon the consequences of such an event, which he does with all his strength, as if by loud sounding words to give battle to his foe* and passionate admonition

---

* This sudden retraction is quite in Shakespeare's manner. Compare " Macbeth," act iv. sc. 3, in which Malcolm " unspeaks his own detraction" to Macduff.

to his patron. The irony in the 4th and 6th lines is self-evident. This is an unusually lucid Sonnet, and the reader will not fail to observe its connection with the 38th, in which the poet appears to have predicted the course events might afterwards take. The 55th, 71st, and 74th spring from the same motive: he does not write for self praise, but to glorify his friend. In the 74th, to which he especially refers, he rejoices that his better parts, when he is dead, will live in his verse, though now he feigns that his friend discards him, and therefore denies without reserve such life, or if his friend desires it he will steal off unidentified and die forgotten.

Sonnet 82.—Since his friend's love for him appears lessened, and he may desire to leave him, the poet at once absolves him from the tie to his verse, by exclaiming—

"I grant, thou wert not married to my Muse;"

and thus fulfils the promise he had made (Sonnet 49), and as he observes his patron desires to give favourable glances to others' dedications, and accept another's love, he admits that he may do so without dishonour, and at once denies the bond of love which united him in marriage of verse with his Muse. His patron had been lauded by an alien pen as one

" Whose outward shape, though it most lovely be,
Doth in fair robes a fairer soul attire;
Who, rich in fading wealth, in endless treasure
Of virtue, valour, learning, richer art, &c.,*

which was certainly a limit beyond Shakespeare's praise.

---

* See Additional Notes. In advanced years (1616) Chapman, in a dedication to him of his translation of Homer, tells him that he is illumined with "the form divine of godlike learning."

His friend's mental graces exceeded his external. Shakespeare never brings them upon the same level. In the 16th his "inward worth" and "outward fair," and in the 54th and other places we find them coupled, though not always to his advantage ; but now in one ironical line more is allowed him by Shakespeare than in all his poem besides. He is told—

"Thou art as fair in knowledge as in hue,"*

or, in other words, as beautiful in mind as in appearance. The patron, esteeming himself of such worth, is obliged to seek some fresher sign of the better new time, foreseen long since (Sonnet 32). After this ironical touch, the poet continues :— And do so love ; yet when they (the rival poets) have done their utmost thy true beauty finds truest sympathy in thy truthful friend. They had better adorn the pallid cheeks of their mistresses with false colourings than thus abuse thee. The closing couplet may be especially compared with the 21st and 67th Sonnets, which bear out the solution here given.

Sonnet 83.—He now excuses himself for having ceased writing, the plea being that his trifling pen fell far short of the excellence the patron deserved, who, being still living, far better published his own growing worth. Thus that which is imputed to Shakespeare as a sin is his chief glory, since by being silent he does not deface beauty, and, promising to give life, bring, like others, a tomb to bury that which exists. This alludes to John

* The quarto, 1609 (the original copy) is printed "hew," and in two places in the 20th Sonnet the word is spelt the same ; it is frequently found so in Spenser and others of that age.

Davies, and the last word of the Sonnet, "devise," may be a pun upon his name. Davies' lines are :—

> "Dear Lord, if so I could I would make known
> How much I long to keep thee still alive ;
> These lines, though short, so long shall be thine own
> As they have power vitality to give."

Davies also extols the friend's "bright eyes;" hence Shakespeare says that the living brightness of the friend's eyes exceeds all that either of his poets can write in his praise. Shakespeare thus excuses his past silence :—I ceased that you might show how vainly a pen of the present time seeks to describe you.

Sonnet 84.—He is asked who is it that says most ? What more can be said than that he is alone himself, and there is no other living like him ? No praise can exceed this ; silence should then ensue, as he himself is the best exposition of himself. The designation of "alien pen" in the 78th, when referring to other poets, is again harped upon in the 5th line of this Sonnet, the conceit lying in the sound of "alien pen" and "a lean pen," which, allied to the expression "lean penury," is peculiarly expressive of the meagre verses to which they refer. But could his rival (the poet adds) describe the patron as he is, the description would be admired by all, and his (*i. e.,* Davies') learning made famous. His fault is that he can neither give glory nor will he let well alone. Shakespeare grieves that such an offering should be accepted, on which account the friend is accused of foolishly loving praise. John Davies, who was a celebrated caligraphist, his skill therein far exceeding his ability to make verses, is here told that he has but to copy what is written in the friend, and his writing will be admired by all.

Sonnet 85.—Shakespeare, however ready to renew his song, will not do so till his rival ceases. He waits attentively, enraptured with the heavenly harmony which he supposes charms his friend, exclaiming :—My mannerly Muse waits patiently while the richest compilation of lasting praise, perfected by all the Muses, is offered to you. While others write good words I think good thoughts, and to every divine hymn that able spirit utters I like an ignorant clerk respond "Amen," thus attesting your praise as truth ; but in thought I add something more, and it but follows by my love for you that it should take the lead. Then esteem others for what they say of you, me for what I think. So that though he had ceased writing to him he had not ceased thinking about him. Poets being formerly termed clerks, the application is thus twofold. "Unlettered" is an ironical re-echo of "rude ignorance" in the 78th. As Davies commenced one of his sonnets with "Dear Lord," he is here pictured as praying for patronage, Shakespeare thus feigning that his rival's love was as devoted as his own—"a religious love." The poet's thoughts, when penning this Sonnet, were apparently dwelling on the encomium Francis Meres had penned upon his verse ; and by recalling to his patron the terms used, thus artfully would mark more vividly the contrast. The passage from the "Wit's Treasury" runs thus :—"As Epius Stolo said the Muses would speak with Plautus' tongue if they would speak Latin, so I say that the Muses would speak with Shakespeare's fine filed phrase if they would speak English."

Sonnet 86.—In the same vein, the poet continues :—

Was it the transcendent merit of his verse directed to you that inhearsed in my brain my mature thoughts? Was it that his spirit was taught by spirits to write above a mortal pitch, that put dead silence upon me? No; my verse was neither astonished at him nor at his mighty familiar (*i. e.*, the spirit of darkness whom he invoked, and who aided him to write above a mortal pitch), and nightly deceived him with false knowledge. He cannot victoriously boast that my silence was through fear; but when your countenance filled up his verse, then I lacked argument. The friend had, as Davies himself intimates, previously accepted his verses—

"Sith once I vowed myself to thee and thine,"

which appears to have been about the time Shakespeare ceased writing, as he feigns that his ripe thoughts were inhearsed in his brain by his rival's lines, which may partly account for the admonition and the abrupt ending of the 77th.

Sonnet 87.—Feigning that his friend will no longer require his unworthy services, he affects to fulfil the promise made in Sonnet 49, and at once bids him farewell. The poet surmises that the friend knows his own worth, which releases him from all the ties with which Shakespeare holds him. The poet is found unworthy of monopolising such a rich gift, and so his patent is withdrawn. It has thus been but a brief delusive dream of friendship, from which he is now awakened. This, it will be found, is in close unity with the 25th, 29th, and 37th Sonnets. At the time Herbert gave himself to Shakespeare he had not, as at this time, by the death of his father in 1601, succeeded to the family titles ; therefore the patron's frailty is imputed to his present high station.

Sonnet 88.—The promise is repeated. The friend is told :—When thou shalt feel disposed to make me appear unworthy, and glance scornfully at my merit, I will attack myself for thy right, and prove thy words true though they are false, knowing well my own unworthiness. Upon thy part I can feign to write of concealed faults wherein I am attainted, that thou by my loss shall win glory, and I too be a gainer ; for my loving thoughts being all thine, the wrongs I do to myself for thy advantage are doubly to my interest, my love for thee being so much thine own that for thy right I will bear all wrong. So he will appear as vile as he presently proves the patron to be for accepting others' praises. The promise the poet makes in this Sonnet is carried out in the 117th.

Sonnet 89.—Assuming that his friend desires entire release from the ties which bind them, the poet will, if his patron so desires it, admit an entire separation. He urges his friend to say that he forsook him for some fault, and he will at once attest the offence. He instances one :—Speak (he tells him) of " my lameness," *i. e.*, impute the worst defects you can to me, and I will make no defence, but will at once deny any claim to thee. Thou canst not, Love (he lovingly exclaims), disgrace me half so vilely by defining the change you desire as I will disgrace myself. Knowing thy wish, I will bring our acquaintanceship to an end, appear a stranger, and be absent from thy company, and my tongue shall cease to utter thy beloved name, lest, being all unworthy, I should shame it by speaking of our former friendship. For thy sake I will debate against myself, for if you hate me I must cease to love myself.

Some have supposed (among them Sir Walter Scott) that Shakespeare was really lame. What excuse would the friend have for leaving him if he was? To sever friendship on that account would indeed be folly. That which the poet means is evident, if we compare with this Sonnet the 36th and 37th, of which this is but a re-echo. We there find that the "lameness" is the separation made between them by fortune; he now refers more especially to the lameness of his verse as an excuse for his patron leaving him.*

Sonnet 90.—If the friend will ever hate him, he is desired to do so now, while the world is disposed to blame him; he is but to join with the spite of fortune, not to delay it; not to give the ominous night of the past a dismal future, causing the poet to live in doubt; not to wait till other comparatively trifling sorrows are past. Let me (says the poet) taste the severest fortune, and what else seems sorrow, will not then be so, compared with thy loss: meaning, that the pangs occasioned by the disgrace the world flings upon him, arising from his disgraced profession, are but slight in comparison to what the loss of his friend would be.

Sonnet 91.—The poet now defines how much he should lose by the loss of his friend. This is a variation of the theme of the 37th, showing how much the covenant of loving friendship obtained for him. All the glory of his friend's youth, beauty, and state he may claim

---

* Shakespeare elsewhere speaks derisively of "a halting Sonnet."

with him. He can then boast of having that which is
the pride of all men, and is only wretched in one thing,
that his friend can take all from him, and make him truly
miserable.*

In the Comedy of "Much Ado about Nothing," there is
passage illustrative of this Sonnet. Benedick, as before
remarked, is unmistakeably a portrait of Herbert, and it
is to him the witty ladies, Beatrice and Margaret, refer in
the ensuing conversation, on the eve of Hero's wedding.
Beatrice exclaims, "Heigh ho!" Margaret demands,
"For a hawk, a horse, or a husband?" She answers,
"For the letter that begins them all, H!" So Shakespeare's heart's desire is for H; and having him, he can
flatter himself he has nobility, beauty, and youth.

Sonnet 92.—The friend is now told that though he
should do his worst to steal himself away; the poet will
claim him for life, and life will stay no longer than his
love; then there is no need of him fearing the worst of
wrongs, when the slightest decay of his friend's love ends
his life. The poet thus fulfils his promise; for though
they are wedded together by verse with the closest of
ties, and it is his privilege to say,

> "For term of life thou art assured mine."

yet, ever ready to bend to his friend's desire, he at once
frees him; the while he will not be cast down, since he
will not observe his inconstancy.

Sonnet 93.—This Sonnet harps upon the concluding

---

* The expressive application of the word "make" in the final line of the
Sonnet is the theme of the three following. Make was formerly synonomous
with husband, i. e., mate. (See allusions in the 4th line of the 9th Sonnet.)

couplet of the foregoing. A reason is given why he should look upon the friend and not detect a fault. Thus shall I live, like a deceived husband (the poet continues), believing you to be true.* I will ever believe your kind looks are towards me, though your heart be elsewhere; by thy loving eye I shall never know the change, nor by thy looks shall I ever know thy heart. Heaven has decreed that love should ever dwell in thy face; and whatever are thy thoughts, or the workings of thy heart, that thy looks should ever declare thee true; but if thy virtue does not equal thy appearance, you will grow like Eve's deceptive apple, rotten at the core; so that, though appearing true in face, the friend would be false in heart.

Sonnet 94,. continues the warning, while covertly alluding to the friend's high station. He is told—Those who have the power of doing injuries, and do none, and do not that which appearances give out, who have the power of moving others, but are themselves unmoved, and are not quickly tempted, are worthy inheritors of heaven's endowments, and husband from waste nature's best gifts; their faces are indexes of their hearts, they being lords of both; others are but stewards, giving an account of their possessions. The summer's flower is sweet to summer, though it lives and dies to itself; but if that flower becomes infected, its worth is exceeded by the basest weed: for as festering lilies smell worse than weeds, so the sweetest by ill deeds become sourest. The friend is thus warned not

---

* The marriage of the muse was also the occasion of the marriage of minds, in which the poet claims his feminine friend in a platonic wedlock, as pictured in Sonnet 20.

to be guilty of the rank fault of deserting him to whom
he is firmly pledged ; and having given himself up to
another, is thus guilty of the vilest connubial sin.   Shakespeare, being complete master of his art, delighted in the
most striking and vivid contrasts, in opposing the brightest
lights to the deepest shades ; more and more fervently he
harps upon the mystic theme, from its lowest note to its
highest pitch.   Upon the present topic—jealousy, the
great dramatist could not lightly speak.   The last line of
this Sonnet appears to have been a proverbial expression ;
there are several such used throughout these Sonnets
and they are also sprinkled throughout the plays.

As a picture of inconstancy in the marriage of minds
it is declared, in the two following Sonnets, that the friend
has become as Eve's apple, and has unfeignedly turned
towards others.   He is accused of the same vice as when
the lady wished to secure him for herself.   These Sonnets
are a climax to the rivalry which the poet has experienced,
the whole of which undoubtedly amused the " private
friends," the language being of such a magical nature
that oftentimes, both with poet and patron, innocence is
made to appear guilt, and the world confounded ; but
anon the poet removes his mask of vice from his picture
of virtue.   The poet, like the Duke in " Measure for
Measure," has an object in view ; for it may be said of
almost all his Sonnets, as of the Duke's missives to
Angelo :—

> " ESCAL. Every letter he hath writ hath disvouched other.
>   ANG. In most uneven and distracted manner.
>   His actions show much like to madness : pray heaven,
>   His wisdom be not tainted."

He does not, as one of Fletcher's characters, " exchange a

real innocence to gain a mere fantastial report," but to fulfil a purpose which we shall fully show.

Sonnet 95.—The poet now, as one of his lordly master's stewards, speaks of himself as recording the story of his patron's early life, and making wanton comments upon his ill behaviour. His vilest faults become him, in him they appear graces; his dispraise becomes praise; his very name is a guard against ill report. Oh! (sighs the poet) thy adulterous friendship makes thee appear but as a mansion inhabited by vices, and though every blot is hid by the veil of beauty, and all things turned fair, beware of thy advantage; you must not belie your appearance: take heed, dear heart, the best tempered steel, ill used, loses its temper; thus apologising for the passionate outburst. The friend now receives the most bitter though loving reproof, because this touched the poet more nearly than the feignings referring to the lady rival.

Sonnet 96.—On the previous occasion of the breach of friendship the friend is forgiven on account of his youth and beauty; he is now pardoned because the poet's rivals are attracted by "his state' and partly on account of the plea others made for him (the private friends), declaring it to be but youthful wantonness. Being alone Shakespeare's, he is warned to be more regardful of his actions, and not to lead away others by making use of his high station, and he is beseeched not to do so, because Shakespeare so loves him by reason of his being his second self that he does not wish by lascivious comments to report ill of him.

The concluding couplet is a repetition of the closing one of the 36th. In the earlier one the poet, fearful lest his friend should become disgraced by him, desired him to rejoice in the separation then occasioned by absence, as the friendship would then bring no disgrace upon him. Now he is blamed for a stain upon his own character. In the earlier one there are fears expressed lest the despised player may disgrace the peer; now the tables are turned, it is the earl who may disgrace the player. This is an apt and loving retort, hence the repetition of the couplet. The friend's fault in the early part of the poem is quickly forgiven, as it is proved to the poet's advantage; but as it is not in the present instance to his honour, the friend is doubly blamed; besides, this apt couplet contains the secret of their mystical union, and the poet repeats the admonition because he is his friend's chronicler, and desires not to allegorise his vices, but to extol his virtues.

These expostulations have the desired effect; reconciliation follows, and no more wanton comments are made upon him, and a far stronger and more lasting friendship grows between them; their ruined love is built anew on a broader principle, and endless peace proclaimed. A retrospect is now given of the poet's past absence, wherein is recapitulated his past and still growing love, and to keep the jest alive the womanly significance of the love the dual Muse entertained for him is again denoted, and the ceremony of love is again renewed, in language at once passionate, delicate, and tender; and as upon their first alliance the sex addressed was undenoted, even so it is upon the renewal of the

song and their reunion, upon which Shakespeare spends
the most honied wedding verse, to celebrate the marriage
of soul to soul and mind to mind, and as testimony that
his love had not lessened.

In the following trio of Sonnets it is indicated that the
cessation of writing was not more than one year, as
surmised in note to Sonnet 77. The poet also intimates
that during the cessation he had been in the intervening
summer widely separated from his friend, probably at
Stratford, and that, being away from his friend, the glory
of the summer seemed but a barren waste.

Sonnet 97.—My absence from thee (the poet exclaims)
hath been like a winter lasting throughout the year.
Yet this cold dark time, when removed from you, was
summer. The plenteous autumn bore in all its rich
abundance the full increase of the prime of summer;
yet all this abounding issue seemed but the prospect of
orphans and unfathered fruit, for thine is the pleasant
summer, and, thou away, the birds either ceased to sing
or sang only in sadness, fearing the winter near. Thus in
the full spirit of parody the poet pourtrays, while relating
his own pangs, the sufferings of an inamorato during a
weary absence. The very seasons appeared to him, when
bereaved of the sunshine of the patron friend, as to the
lover; and the birds on this account were mute or sang
in sadness, therefore his own silence may be fully
forgiven.

Sonnet 98.—Though absent in the propitious spring,
when all nature and all things seemed gladdened, the
poet was borne down by a weight of care; in him alone
the spirit of youth was wanting. His friend absent from
his verse, he could not write gladsomely, nor did he care

to pluck the gay flowers fresh from the lap of Flora. To beguile the weary time he compared the sweet flowers with his sweeter friend; yet it still seemed winter, and, his friend being absent, he addressed them as being his similitude. Being but poor shadows of him, he makes them his sport. The poet thus hints that he had retired from the metropolis to his native place, as was his custom, to write for the stage; but, in the words of Brathwaite, he feared "his 'Midsummer Night's Dream' was but a 'Winter's Tale.'"

Sonnet 99.—Thus he chided the forward violet :— From whom hast thou stolen thy sweet smell, if not from the breath of my loved friend? The proud purple complexion dwelling on thy soft cheek thou hast too deeply empurpled in my love's veins.* The lily he blamed as less fair than his friend's hand, and the marjoram buds had stolen the softness of his hair. The roses on thorns fearfully stood; one blushed with shame, another white with envy; a third, neither red nor white, had stolen of both, to which robbery he added his breath, and for his theft, in spite of all his show, a vengeful canker was destroying him. The poet observed other flowers, but saw none but what had stolen sweet or colour from his friend. Thus even the red rose, the favourite of his song, blushed with disgrace, but the white utterly despaired.

From this point the Muse is ever and anon chided for having left the friend, her all the world, for the world, which is nothing in respect of the friend.

In the two following Sonnets the poet divides himself

---

* See Sonnet 20, the poet defeated by nature.

from his other self, his Muse, and calls his friend his own love, because she, by neglecting her beloved, is supposed to love the less. From this charge she defends herself in the 102nd.

Sonnet 100.—The poet now accuses his Muse of forgetfulness in having for some time ceased to speak of that which gave her all her power. Is she spending her fury on some worthless song (referring to his remark in Sonnet 98, line 7), casting a shade upon her glory, lending unworthy subjects light (*i. e.*, writing for the public) ? Let her return, and at once redeem her idly spent time, sing to the ear that esteems her lays* and gives to her tongue both skill and argument. Rise (he says), Muse, weary of rest, survey my sweet love's face ; if any mark of time appears, satirise decay, and make the defacings of time everywhere despised. Give my love fame faster than time destroys the living, that thou mayest oppose his destructive scythe's oblivion, and his crooked (*i. e.*, marring) knife's defacings. Shakespeare thus flatters the unrivalled strength of his Muse to induce her to renew her efforts ; he also hints that the friend's beauty is now at the best, or may soon pass its prime ; but as the Muse does not observe a wrinkle she does not pen a satire on decay.

Sonnet 101.—The muse is again personally rebuked, and the fault of silence is imputed to her ; she has forgotten her beloved task. What shall be her recompense

---

* See Additional Notes to this Sonnet, extract from a poem by Chettle on the death of Queen Elizabeth. Shakespeare is blamed for refraining from writing an ode to her memory. It appears as if he had Chettle's poem before him when writing the above to the sovereign of his own choice.

for neglecting beauty's truthful rose? As truth and
beauty receive their glory from his friend, so by him is
his muse dignified. She may perchance excuse her silence
by saying that truthful beauty needs no colouring, and
that best is best; but this will not avail, she is told to
fulfil her task, and to make him long outlive a gilded
tomb, and appear to future ages as he now appears. The
Muse perchance discovers his beauty is unimpaired by
time, and may say he needs not her painted praise to
revive it; and though the poet is willing to pursue the
song, the Muse upon her part having fulfilled her office,
though unwilling to proceed, at once pens her sweetest
love lines.

Sonnet 102.—She apologises by comparing her love
with that of others who have addressed the patron, and
published the offerings of their pens for self profit. She
was wont before they appeared to sing lays upon their
love. It was then new and in its spring; and as the
nightingale who sings in the early summer, ceases to
sing in mellower days, not that the summer is less
pleasant than when her plaintive hymns lulled the night,
but that every bough is burdened with wild music now,
and sweets, become common, are less delightful; so she, of
late has held her tongue, lest her songs should become
wearisome. The song of the poet's Muse, like the
nightingale's, ceased to contend with the common herd;
and though her love has not appeared so strong as upon
the celebration of their unity, yet in this, the summer of
their love, it has increased rather than diminished.

Sonnet 103.—Having written one of her best Sonnets,

the poet speaks of his Muse's effort with feigned contempt
and rebuke, because she will not retouch the portrait she
has drawn so well, and as an excuse for her ceasing
singing, he apologises for her, and reminds his friend that
she had not ceased the song till she had accomplished her
object, and that he now is best, as he is without art's
adornment ; and if he is not dulled by the song, the song
is dulled by the better reflection of him which his glass
will present. All this is but a variation of L'Envoy
(77), the termination of the first part ; and, as before
shown, the song was prolonged only at the patron's instigation. In the sixth couplet, Shakespeare states that his
sole object is to tell of his friend's graces and gifts,
which has been fulfilled as far as the Muse's power would
admit of : her office was to portray the beauty of his
spring, the fresh May morn of his days ; in the next he
refers to the brief time this season exists.

Sonnet 104.—Having intimated that the friend had
now become a man, and that consequently his freshest
beauties were leaving him, which he might himself discover, the poet says—To me, beautiful friend, you will
never appear old, for as you were when first my eye
viewed yours, such you seem still, though three cold
winters have shaken three summers' pride from the
forest, and three beauteous springs have turned to yellow
autumn ; though in the seasons change I have seen three
fragrant Aprils burned in three hot Junes, since first I saw
you fresh, who art still green ; ah ! yet doth beauty, like
a dial-hand, steal from thy face, and no change is perceived ;
so your sweet hue, which methinks still remains, hath

motion, and mine eye may be mistaken. Lest it is so, hear this, thou unborn age, ere you lived, beauty's summer died.

The allusion is to the time when the poet first saw him a boy, prior to the date of the commencement of the song, when first he recorded his bright eyes and fair hue, which still stand fresh in his verse. Thus, now circa 1603-4 refers to 1597-8, the date of the first Sonnet, from which date Time has been withheld. He reminds his friend he first saw him three years before this date 1597-8, *i.e.* in 1594-5, and resolves to consider him still as young, and give him an eternal youth. Three years would not cause so much change in the boy's aspect, but nearly nine years, the actual period, might produce the difference. The poet in the first 77 Sonnets celebrated youthful, manly beauty; and now, though the friend declines from the top of happy hours, the poet lovingly sees him in the ascendant, such as he first saw him three years before 1598, and the song in this spirit is concluded. He is not spoken of as the man of the opening Sonnets, but as the "lovely boy" of their first acquaintanceship. In 1595, Master Herbert was at Oxford completing his studies, and probably their first meeting was there, and as there is a tradition that Shakespeare visited this city on his way to the metropolis from his native town, it tends to confirm the supposition. The poet also denotes this date by reminding him that the reference is not to the time of their having first become friends, but to the time he first beheld him, wherever it might have been, as a bright-eyed youth. It will be observed that the poet does not in this renewal descant as hitherto on his own years, but upon the advancing years of his friend; for as he denotes in Sonnet 110, this revival gives his heart "another youth." There was no occasion to again dilate upon the theme of age and death; in the former part he had said all he had to say upon that subject.

Sonnet 105.—The unborn age mentioned in the last, is not to call the love of the Muse idolatry, nor her beloved an idol, because she is true to one that is true, and whose beauty is true; he is both truly beautiful, truly loving, and truly constant; and she contends three such virtues never before dwelt in one; and it may be said to her honour, she never offered panegyrics to any other; the prostitution of praise offended her.

Sonnet 106.—A backward look is now given into the chronicles of the past, to discover if there is record of any other of such worthiness. It is found that writers of antiquity would have expressed such beauty as he masters now, and, as in Sonnet 59, to which this is a decided answer, through his dual nature, all praise ever penned to ladies dead, or lovely knights, he is alone entitled to.* All their praises were but prophecies prefiguring him, though neither the ancients nor the moderns can rightly sing his praise.† The poet evidently viewed these poems as something more than parodies; as before denoted, they are art's offering at the shrine of beauty. The opening lines of this Sonnet appear to refer to the rhymed romances of the French and Italian poets. The term "ladies dead" may refer to those idealized ladies, Beatrice

---

* The fourth line of the last Sonnet and the fifth in this are wedded together, the one begetting the other.

† This is a further excuse for ceasing the song, all eyes admire him, but no tongue can praise him sufficiently.

and Laura, these ladies being sonnetted after their deaths by both their poet lovers.

In the next he asserts, in self vindication, that his love is not confined to a limited period, but is of endless date.

Sonnet 107.—Having looked into times past, he now looks into times present. If the poet affects to fear his verse cannot praise his friend to his desire, he relies upon its endurance, as upon his own love. He speaks thus in favour of the constancy of his love and verse—I have no fear that coming events will alter my vow, or that the lease of my love will end ; my friendship will endure in spite of death itself, nor is it affected by passing circumstances. The mortal moon (Elizabeth) has suffered eclipse (died 24th of March, 1603, between the cessation and renewal of the song, which may have begun again in the April following), and the serious augers, *i.e.*, the poet's envious detractors, are deceived in their foolish guesses, in supposing the friendship was ended with the cessation of address. Doubts are now ended, the poet has proved the friend's sincerity, by his friend desiring him to renew the address, and mutual peace is ever more agreed upon. Now, he continues, in this most joyful time, my love I still behold young, and death submits to me, since, in spite of him, I and my friend shall live in this poor rhyme, while he tyrannises over tyrants, and those not blessed by the voice of poetry. The moon's eclipse (Elizabeth's death) is followed by (this most balmy time) . the sunrise of the accession of James.* This is also to be looked upon as an excuse for the Muse to cease her song ; her task is now accomplished, her love still looks

---

* See additional notes to Sonnet 107, as to Pembroke's joy on the accession of James.

young. Time thus submits to her power, and oblivious
death is defeated. This Sonnet appears to be imitated in
one by Drayton, upon the alterations made by Time,
"since first his love began," in which mention is made of
the "quiet end of that long living queen" and "this
king's fair entrance."

Having so oft repeated what has before been said, the poet
demands in the next what more he can say—whether still to
address his friend as the beautiful boy he first saw him, now
time and outward form belie his words ? No! he will then
speak of himself, and no more addresses his friend as such,
till he arrives at the L'Envoy, and to keep his plea good
though finally addressing him as a boy, alters the form
of the Sonnet, so that though to him, it virtually belongs
not to the series.

The song of friendship having commenced with an
overture of Seventeen Sonnets, when the youth was
seventeen, the concert being brought to a happy termination, is now finished with a voluntary of the same number
the song opened with, in which the poet speaks as much
of himself as he did of the friend in the beginning ; and the
following is the poet's most solemn plea for ending the
song of praise.

Sonnet 108.—Continuing the plea for the Muse, he
says—Now, when so much is done, what more need be
said ? What is there to say, sweet boy ? There is
nothing ! Then, if all is said, must I repeat the same
daily, like a divine prayer ? Must I still say, you are
young, as of old, and not consider you are daily growing older, I first loved you for the beauty of your

youth, but time and outward appearance prove you are
not youthful now? This plea is deemed all sufficient,
and having alluded to the first address, wherein he styled
him beauty's rose, he in the next asserts that though he
has been a traveller since then, he is still his Muse's all in
all—her most beloved rose.

Sonnet 109.—Now all is done, the friend is told he is
never more to doubt the poet's actions, either of the past
or the future ; and as he has lasciviously commented upon
the friend's assumed adultery of friendship, he now also
vindicates what has been supposed vile in his own conduct. He thus begins—Oh! never say that my heart
was false, though absence seemed to subdue my passion ;
as easy might I depart from myself, as from my soul,
which lies in thy breast (Sonnet 22), that is its abode.
If I have ranged (which cannot be) like a traveller, I
return again, still sincere, not changed with the time,
so that I wash away my guilt. Never believe, though
my nature were governed by all the frailties of mankind,
that it could so outrageously be stained, as to leave for
nothing all thy goodness ; for to thee the universe is
nothing, thou art my all in all. The absence giving rise
to the appearance of coldness was the poet's only fault.
In the following Sonnets, he intimates that the friend's
pure flame was not subdued. In the next, he admits
in sadness having left him, how he spent the time, and
its most joyful results.

Sonnet 110.—Alas! I have gone from place to place,*

---

* Probably referring to the Globe and Blackfriars Theatres, of both of
which he was a shareholder, and at both of which he had appeared upon
the stage.

the poet continues (giving to others your time), arrayed to public view in garments of varied stain, wounding my thoughts, selling cheap that (my reputation) which is most dear, anew offending my better judgment. It is also most true that I have viewed askance, and strangely thy truth (Sonnet 101), *i.e.*, not devoted myself fully to you ; but by all above these frailties gave my heart a fresh youth (the song being renewed to the youth of former days) and worst trials have proved thee my best friend. Now all is done, accept my love without end, for never-more will I seek new friends, to try the patience of my old one ; a god in love, to whom I am entirely given up, then accept my heart's offering, and place it in the heaven of thy bosom. In the 109th, they were again said to be one ; in this, by being so, the poet is no more old, but receives by this return a new youth, though an older friend.

He now pens the climax to the undignified publicity, first touched upon in Sonnet 29.

Sonnet 111.—O, for my sake, accuse fortune, the guilty goddess,* the cause of my ill deeds, (compelling the poet to leave his friend for the public), that did not provide better for my life than public means, which breed public manners ; thence comes it that my name is branded, and almost thence my nature is reduced to the level of its grade, being stained, like a dyer, with my avocation. Pity me then, and desire me cleansed, while I, a willing patient, will drink the bitterest potions, and no penance will I think too severe to be absolved. Pity me then, dear

---

† The "guilty goddess," the occasion of all his sorrows, is thus contrasted with his friend, "a god in love," the cause of all loving joy.

friend, and that alone will cure me. The friend doing so, he will never more regret the public shame.

In the 110th he is renewed in youth, in this he desires to be renewed from the stains so much lamented. He may also refer to the plague which was raging in London in 1603, if so, the language would be peculiarly appropriate. It is known that after this date the poet appeared no more upon the stage, and from 1597 to this date, he but on particular occasions appeared on the public stage. About 1604, the Earl of Pembroke was offended at young Massinger, a son of one of his father's chief retainers, for following dramatic writing, instead of the law, upon which the Earl withdrew his patronage, and Massinger left college. The theatric festivities the young student had witnessed at Wilton, may have first inspired him to become a votary of the muses. Shakespeare, for these reasons, may thus speak of his own actions and writings in such terms. We may also infer from the apparent disregard he evinced for his plays in regard to their publication, and the not altogether feigned sorrow he here expresses at his fate, that he thought fortune might have used his genius better, in this opinion he was not alone.

Sonnet 112.—The request being tendered, he is absolved from these compelled sins of his life. The love and pity of his patron ennobles his brow, and erases the brand vulgar scandal stamped upon it. Then what cares he for the opinion of others? since his friend puts a good colour upon his bad, and approves his good. Hence he puts the world into his friend's person, and by him alone will he be judged. To both critic and flatterer he turns a deaf ear. His friend being so replete to his purpose, he will believe all others are naught.

Sonnet 113.—The four foregoing Sonnets open the poet's vindication ; the ensuing four recount his devotedness during absence, his increased love, and how it remained a fixed star during his wanderings. He begins by declaring that his mind's eye had ever presented the image of his friend to view, continually keeping him in remembrance. He is so much his all the world that his eye converts every object to his resemblance. His eye was intoxicated with the excess of beauty, though not as Spenser said of a knight whose eye was enthralled by wantonness :—

" Made drunk by drugs of dear voluptuous receipt."

It is such whom Shakespeare, in majestic language, thus covertly satirises. The reader will not fail to observe that the poet harps upon the similarity of sound in " mine " and " my eyne " in the last line of the Sonnet.

Sonnet 114.—It is doubtful whether his speaking eye saith (a pun on seeth) true, or whether his great mind loves flattery. He saith that his eye loves flattery, and prepares the delicious cup for his kingly mind to drink up. If it be poisoned, the sin is less, his eye loving it reflects its love upon his great mind. Thus he has charged himself with a sin of a parallel tendency to the one (Sonnet 84) imputed to the friend. In this double Sonnet the poet evidently parodies such sonnetteering as Spenser's 86th.

Sonnet 115.—Those lines written before the renewal of their love " do lie ;" thus the poet's eye and mind and tongue are alike proved innocently false. The avowals of love his pen had uttered were all too weak ; but then he knew not that the lamp of love, though burning brightly, might afterwards burn clearer. Thinking of the many accidents that happen as time advances, creeping in betwixt vows and changing the decrees of kingly minds (alluding to their seemingly severed vows and changed decrees), staining with age holy beauty (Sonnets 68 and 104), turning aside the strongest minds to change with changing things, fearing time's changeful tyranny, might he not then say :—Now I love you best. Doubtful of the future, he is, however excused. Love being a babe, he might then say so, giving full growth to that which is still growing ?

Assuming that the foregoing may amount to an admittance that love when urged to the extreme may be compelled to alter, that he neither has nor will know change is the purport of the following Sonnet, in which he alludes to the vow and decree which bound them together in a religious friendship.

Sonnet 116.—Arrived at the crowning height of the Epithalamium in mutual purity, the poet might well exclaim : — Let me not admit impediments to the marriage of true minds (*i. e.*, unalterable friendship). Love is not love that alters as events alter. Oh, no ! it is ever fixed, come what will ; it is never shaken ; it is the guiding star to every wandering bark (Sonnet 117, Shakespeare himself) whose worth is unknown, although his dimensions may be taken. Love is not the fool of Time, though rosy lips and cheeks come within his bending sickle's compass ; nor is it altered by brief hours and weeks, but is borne out to the end of time. If this be not so and proved upon me, neither I ever writ nor man ever loved. He thus proves that friendship, like marriage, is made for life, or, as Cæsar said, " the die is cast." Neither the spiteful misrepresentations of others, who, as will be seen, slandered him to his patron, or the poet's own groundless jealousies and suspicions, were permitted to dissolve the bond of faithful loving friendship.

Sonnet 117.—Assuming that this may be thought more than truth, the friend is told to charge the poet as appearances gave out, that he might at once make a plea;* the friend is told to accuse him of neglect in repaying the rich merit as he deserved, of being forgetful of the loving bond of fellowship which united them, of having given to unknown minds, *i.e.*, to the public, the time and the society which were the due of one alone, whom he should have invoked daily as the tenth Muse, to charge him with setting sail to all the winds which should transport him furthest from his friend's sight. His friend is bid to frown upon him, not to be suddenly wrathful against him, since the defence that he will make is that he but strove to test the virtues and constancy of his friendship. The poet is now commenting upon his own (allegorical) lasciviousness. This is in contrast to Sonnet 40, last couplet. He would not then be his friend's foe ; his friend must not now be his.

In the next he descants upon the means he took to try his goodness.

Sonnet 118.—The poet and his Muse being one, he

---

* Since he resolves to make no more vindications or palliations, when this series is ended.

now speaks in his own name of her having been sick
(Sonnet 79), asserting that it arose from excess of love,
which forms another plea for the silence, in which love,
as in Sonnets 56 and 75, is compared to appetite. Being
full of never cloying sweet friendship (Sonnet 75), he
thought it policy to put it to the trial when there was no
occasion, that he might enjoy his friend's sweet society
better after bitter separation, even as we use medicine
when in health to avoid sickness. The poet, however,
finds, and need no more repeat the lesson, that the drugs
taken to cure his love sickness were considered poison
ending their love. This especially refers to the delightful
intercourse the wished-for meeting occasioned, which was
a surfeit of love, of which the Muse he feigns fell sick.

Sonnet 119.—The Muse's ravings during absence are
now depicted,* and thus, in the masquerade of language,
are pictured a lover's maddening forebodings during
absence. The course of medicine is now described, and
its effects. She has imbibed deeply of siren tears, being
the distillation of a hell of thought, giving fears to hopes,
and hopes to fears, still fearing to lose him she had ever
won. What wretched errors for the heart to commit
when it thought itself never so blest, arising from cause-
less doubt, starting her eyes from their spheres in this
maddening fever's distraction. But thence she learns—oh,
benefit of ill! that which was before good is still bettered
by evil, and renewed love becomes stronger and greater
than at first; so she returns gladly rebuked, since she
gains by it thrice more than was spent in tearful separation. Her offence is, then, an advantage, as it occasions
an increase of love.

---

* Alluding to the mistress series.

Sonnet 120.—A plea is now made for mutual forgiveness, as they have each been assumed guilty of the crime of frailty in friendship ; so it is now to the poet's benefit that the friend was once faithless, since they prove alike guilty—on the one side for ceasing to write, on the other for accepting the love of another (Sonnets 33 and 43). If the friend has felt the pangs of neglect as much as the Muse then did his crime, he has passed an insupportable time ; but as the Muse has by silence been most in error, she is the first to ask forgiveness, and as they have each transgressed they must pardon each other. The reader will not fail to observe that the "night of woe" and the "dark days" of the 97th refer to one and the same event ; and, as in Sonnet 34, the friend sought pardon from the poet for his trespass, so now the Muse seeks pardon of the friend ; and as the Muse freely forgave her beloved's severest wrong, so he must now forgive her, as she, a tyrant to herself, seeks not to show how much she then suffered.

A final and complete vindication is now written. It is levelled at those who have accused him to his patron of having been guilty of the crime of frailty in friendship, which he has so grievously acknowledged, but shown it to be on account of the constrained blemishes of fortune. The accusation is now turned against his accusers, it being the base only who believe all men are, like themselves, base. He urges if others (the evil augurs of Sonnet 109) choose to consider him a wayward unloving friend, he cares not for their thoughts, he knows himself best, let them look to themselves. The Sonnet, divested of allegory, is thus rendered.

Sonnet 121.—It were better I had been frail to you and enjoyed the pleasure of other friendships, than not to have been fickle and yet be esteemed so by jealous observers. Why should their false eyes see in me such inconstancy? Or if I have proved so, why am I accused by others far worse, who in their thoughts reckon that (the absence and neglect) bad, which I think good? (See Sonnet 119.) No; I am that I am, *i. e.*, constant and unalterable, and the crime they charge me with, they are guilty of themselves. I may be true, though they be false; my deeds must not be judged by their gross thoughts, unless they can prove that all men are alike guilty, and live triumphing in it. If so, and his friend does not forgive him, it were better he became as wayward as others, and not be falsely esteemed so.

Sonnet 122.—The poet now confesses himself guilty of a fault, but proves it not to be one. He appears to have received, in return for the present he made (Sonnet 77) a gift of memorandum tablets. The poet, to his patron's surprise, and his enemies' delight, bestowed the gift on another, for which he purposed making this complimentary excuse :—I had no need for thy gift of tables, so I gave them to another, as I have you fixed past erasure upon the far more enduring tablets of my brain and heart. It would denote forgetfulness in me to carry tables to keep thee in remembrance. They were possibly too costly for use, and the poet cared not to retain any such outward sign of remembrance of that love ever fixed upon his brain and heart; hence he considered it a mark of truer love to part with them, perhaps to another who needed them more. May not this have been the lady rival ? She might be assumed to require them more than the Muse.

Sonnet 123.—A final declaration is now made to Time, with whom he has warred and come off victorious, and who would therefore rejoice to see the poet's protestations fail. He vauntingly challenges him to show among the wonders of the world ('Time's registers), anything so lasting as the poet's newly erected verse (the poet's register). He instances the foremost of Time's trophies— the Pyramids, exclaiming—No! Time thou shalt not boast that I do change ; thy pyramids rebuilt with greater strength (referring to his love), would occasion no surprise in me. They would be but that which has been before ; our lives being brief, we admire the things palmed upon us as old, and remain in doubt as to the date of their origin and ending. I defy both thee and thy registers, and am neither astonished at what has been or what still exists ; for thy trophies, as those which have been, will become razed ; as you hasten onward they continually change, but I vow that for ever I will remain unchanged, regardless of thee and thy scythe.

Sonnet 124.—Continues extolling this erection of love and verse, denoting that it was built on a firm basis, and cannot be overthrown, and is not like others short lived. He then continues—If my dear love were but the offspring of ceremony, it might, as a bastard of fortune, be un-fathered, being subject to love or hate as time offered, receiving hate in hate, and love in love. No! it was built beyond the chance of such accident ; it is neither exalted by smiling pomp, nor becomes a ruin hurled down by discontent, which is the fashion of these times. It fears not faithless policy, which soon comes to an end, but stands by itself, hugely politic ; it is the same in the warmth of love, as in the storms of hate. To this I am witness, and calls those friendships the fools of time, which begin and end for self-interest, and but exist for this crime.

In the next, he makes a final and serious apology for ceasing writing, his plea being that he has seen others lose everything by offering too much.

Sonnet 125.—We now come to the ending protestation, it is a variation of the 25th, and takes up the theme of the last, in which he defines other's friendships as short-lived fallacies, compared to his own. He further weighs the advantages, assuming that his love was but as theirs is at the best. He exclaims—What were it to me if " I bore the canopy," *i.e.*, were one of mere outward ceremony of friend-ship, or sought to build an eternal love upon such a basis, and thus fall far short of the intent ? Have I not seen dwellers upon form and favour lose more than all by offering too much, while existing upon a passing smile. Pitiful thrivers, gazing is their all. No ! I will not be such : let my heart be placed in thy heart ; take the offering, poor, but given freely, my pure undivided love, without guile, only mutual, render me for thee. Henceforth, thou perjurer (to the person who falsely accused him to his friend as faithless, see Sonnets 107 and 121), a truthful soul when tested to the utmost stands free from thy slanderous charges. In the concluding lines, Shakespeare imitates, or rather parodies, Spenser's 89th Sonnet, which is addressed in the bitterest language to one who had spoken falsely of him to his love. The poet thus concludes, by asserting that from this time they shall be no more divided, hence there is no more need of sonnetting.

We have now arrived at the conclusion of the poem; and more especially to mark its distinctive ending, this L'Envoy is written in half a dozen couplets. The friend is gently warned, both as the boy of their first acquaintanceship, resplendent with youth and beauty, and as the full grown man of the present time. Like the theme, it is a complete inversion, and may be thus rendered.

Sonnet 126.—O thou, my lovely boy, who hast the power to hold the sickle, glass, and fickle hour of Time, who hast gone back while advancing, by which thou observest thy lovers withering* while thou art growing; if Nature, mistress of us all, will still, as I do, hold thee back as thou goest forward, it is for this purpose she keeps thee young, that these times of adulterous art may be disgraced by her skill,† and triumph over wretched minutes. Yet take heed, thou sport of her pleasure; she may detain, though still not keep thee; and though her final account is delayed, it must be answered, and when she renders thee her chief glory she will be silent, for all is ended. He shows that Nature, like the Muse, will lose her best subject.

---

* See Sonnets 1 and 10. The song thus ends attesting that fatherly love for his friend which has been repeatedly expressed throughout the poem; the one has gained a lost son, the other a lost father. In Sonnet 37 the poet alludes to his having lost his son Hamnet, "the crutch of his age." Herbert now supplies his place, he is the support of his years.

† See Sonnets 67 and 68.

K

SONNETS 127 TO 154,

FORMING THE COMPANION PICTURE TO THE FOREGOING SONNETS.*

" Hearts remote, yet not asunder."—*Phœnix and Turtle.*

" Who shall compare love's mean and gross desire
   To the chaste zeal of friendship's sacred fire ?
   By whining love our weakness is confest,
   But stronger friendship shows a virtuous breast." –*Massinger.*

                    " How can I, then, be free
   To love another, having once loved thee ?"—*Pembroke's Poems.*

                    " My friend and I are one :
   Sweet flattery ! then she loves but me alone."—*Shakespeare's Sonnet* 42.

" Sweet beauty hath no name, no holy hour,
   But is profaned, if not lives in disgrace."—*Shakespeare's Sonnet* 127.

                    " Had I not vowed to confine
   Myself to no more wives than only nine,
   Parnassus brood."—*Randolph.*

IN the poem to the friend, he is upbraided for turning
from his allegiance to Shakespeare's Muse for the love of
a mistress ;† in these succeeding Sonnets the poet
upbraids the mistress for stealing his friend from him,
and this in far bitterer terms than he had blamed his
friend, in consequence of the love the Muse had for the

---

* Though these Sonnets as will be shown were written to Herbert's Mistress they were covertly levelled at Lady Rich, " the fair woman with a dark
soul," whom Sidney had previously sonnetted as an angel of perfection ;
and though allegorical with regard to the mutual loving, were intended to
be literal satires on this notable frail married lady, and on the times.

† The term mistress is here used by Shakespeare as denoting " a woman
beloved and courted."

friend being of the closest and most tender kind. It may be thought that the allegory was of such a nature as to be unfit for a pure lady's ear; but if the reader turns to the works of our poet he will find some of the purest and loveliest of Shakespeare's heroines use similar language. The times are changed since then, and we are more scrupulous, but perhaps no purer. What should we now say to the ladies Beatrice and Helena? The former would speak of these Sonnets, if she had had the key, knowing they were allegorical, and to be applied literally to another, as all " mirth and no matter ;" and what maiden would now discourse upon virginity to a soldier as Helena does to Parolles? In these Sonnets to the mistress it is the poet who speaks in allegory, in the dramas it is the ladies who speak in unadorned simplicity; hence that which Shakespeare wrote, though to a pure lady, in those plain spoken times might have been well received. The first eighteen of these Sonnets bear internal evidence of having been written during the first journey from the friend. Thus in Sonnet 144 the poet speaks of the friend and the mistress being " both from me," and several of the earliest of these Sonnets are but variations of the theme of Sonnets 33 to 43, and in the 152nd Sonnet the language used is the exact counterpart of that used in the 41st. The 143rd, too, seems a natural reference to the 37th. In the poem to the friend, the simile used is a "decrepid father"—a man; in that to the mistress the simile used is a "careful housewife"—a woman.

Besides being apparently written to abuse the friend's mistress, the poet had in view a higher and more difficult object: he designed to paint the great vice of the times

—incontinence in wedded life—in the black terms it deserved, as if to brand the times, at which he has so much railed in the poem to the friend. That this scheme would please the patron is evident from the poems written by Lord Herbert himself, for he eventually became a votary of the Muses;* and as the patron's taste lay that way, so also his servant Shakespeare moulded his verse. The poet being himself married (allegorically, in mind) to the friend, turns round upon the mistress who has seduced him, and under the guise of upbraiding her, has left a picture of the times in which he lived. Smarting under the wrong his friend had done him, and for which he had forgiven him, he pictures the mistress who had taken his friend from him, and the occasion of wrong in one is the occasion of mutual implication, but the poet ends by proving himself to be the most blameworthy for loving her after her ill deed. The friend, as Sonnets 1 and 10 denote, reserved his love for the poet alone, and up to the 32nd kept it for Shakespeare's Muse only. For this reason, Shakespeare paints the mistress in the darkest colours, and commences sonnetting her as the symbol of the adulterous art and profanity of her sex, though finally he palliates her offence by turning the blame upon himself. With these remarks, we proceed to the first address to her, which commences by the poet speaking of her as his own, which is true, not only according to the "sweet flattery" of the 42nd Sonnet, but also with the ending of the poem (Sonnet 125), in which the poet and his friend are made anew but one

---

* Wood says this earl was not only a favourer of learned and ingenious men, but was also himself endowed to admiration with a poetical genius.

person. He commences by way of prologue, with up-braiding the women of the age.

Sonnet 127.—It would appear from this Sonnet that the friend's mistress was a dark lady, and the most is certainly made of her black complexion; but it is her deeds alone that give rise to this assumed blackness (Sonnet 131), or, as explained in a line by Marlowe—

" Now inward faults thy outward form disgrace,"

though she was evidently a brunette, with very dark star like eyes and dark brown hair, besides which, it was customary to speak of those with such hair and eyes as black. She it is who was the dark cloud of the 33rd Sonnet that obscured thebright friend from the poet. Compared to the Muse, to whom the friend is virtuously allied, and who was, of course, of radiant brightness, the lady may well be said to have been pre-eminently black; and as the poem to the friend commenced by praising the friend's eyes, so he commences hers by praising her eyes. They are raven black, and her brows are arrayed in the same hue, which makes them appear like lovely mourners, grieving for those who are not born beautiful, yet are in no want of beauty, since they disgrace creation with false show; and it is so becoming of her thus to appear to mourn, that all extol her as beauty's self.

As before observed in preliminary observations, we find in one of our poet's earliest plays, that the witty Biron loved to flout at sonnetteering, and in some conceited lines, he speaks in the same paradoxical manner of his mistress, black being fair, as the poet does in this Sonnet. From this it may be inferred, that as beauty was profaned by woman, the poet has given the praise to man, even to such a one as St. Gregory would have termed an "angel friend." Thus he may well, now beauty is desecrated, lament that in woman it has "no holy hour," which stands in contrast to Sonnet 68. Hence the friend is pictured fair, the mutual mistress dark; she is to be the emblem of the profanity and corruption of the age, and yet, when divested of the surrounding allegorical vesture, like the friend, she stands revealed as beautiful and as pure as Imogen.

Her mournfulness is much dilated upon in this and the following Sonnet, to which those tearful Sonnets, the 33rd, 34th, and 35th, among others, are especially referable. In those, it is the tears of the lady-love that are pearls, and are sufficient atonement for both her fault and the friend's. The poet thus rejoices in her sorrow, she is forgiven, and he commences sonnetting her upon it; though it is manifest, that even while the poet was pursuing the mystical conceit, he freely forgave her from the first; but because she will not love and pity him, he affects not to do so. His entreaty for her love and pity arises in the desire that she will assume he is her real lover, just as he assumes she is his real mistress, and make, as he himself does, his loss gain. As the poet, upon the first alliance by verse, viewed the friend as his own, so upon the friend allying himself with the lady, the poet viewed her as his own, and addressed her as such. In Sonnet 36, addressing his friend, he says, We two are twain, but " our undivided loves are one;" and in the 38th Sonnet, we are told that the friend was the originator of the conceit.* This Sonnet,

* And it is highly probable he conceived the idea of satirising by this

and all up to the 144th, were written and sent at the same time, as the ten detailing the same event, to the friend. The poet has thus made this in direct contrast to the first Sonnet in the first series ; and it is written in her praise on account of the sweet flattery that his friend and himself are but one, and that she alone loves him.

Sonnet 128.—The poet now, in the name of his friend as her lover, makes a lawful demand. The lady, who appears to have been a player upon the virginal, seems to have ravished the poet with harmony, which he has infused in the Sonnet. He prettily quibbles on jacks, the keys of the instrument, and Jack's meddlers, to whom she offers her hands to kiss, but a real lover desires and deserves to kiss her lips. In the 5th couplet, he makes allusion to having changed his state and situation by impersonating the friend ; nevertheless, he does not get more than her hand to kiss, and is no better off than the "saucy Jacks," though he ought as the friend to reap the harvest from her lips. The poet would have continued to address his friend's lady-love in this pleasing strain, had he not had in view a far higher purpose ; yet the Sonnet has its object, it reminds her of the time when the poet was with her in happy innocence, before she had wantonly sought to win his friend from his Muse.

Sonnet 129.—Having described her beauty and accomplishments, he pictures allegorically the sin of this loving delusion ; he sees the futility of seeking to possess her love alone, illicit love is despised as soon as possessed, yet he

marriage allegory, that Comet of ill-omen as she has been called, the disgrace at once of Sidney the Pembrokes, and the Court of Elizabeth.

excuses this delusive dream—he like all the world is enthralled by love.

He denounces their mutual sin, to induce the mistress to
give up the friend, who is already married to Shakespeare's
Muse, and thus cannot, without a threefold crime, be
another's. By her love for the friend she is thus the innocent occasion of their mutual sin. This stands as prologue, and epitomises the argument which follows—its
theme being infidelity in love.

Sonnet 130.—A satirical picture of the mistress, in contrast to the high-flown terms used by the sonnetteers of
the day, and is referable to the 21st, to the friend. This the
poet asserts in the person of the friend, and, while acknow-
ledging her to be but an ordinary mortal, she is said,
nevertheless, to be as rare as the goddesses of others,
belied by false comparisons. This, of course, is a totally
opposite picture to what she really was. Nevertheless,
in the following, she is said to be like other beauties,
proudly cruel ; so that, apart from the allegorical disguise,
the poet has both the best of friends and the best of
mistresses.

Sonnet 131.—The lady still keeps the friend, in despite
of which the poet, in the name of his friend, confesses his
love for her ; and though she is blamed by others (as
personating Lady Rich in the vale of years), and said
to be unworthy of love, he will think her the best, in
spite of being the worst (through taking the friend),
it being her deeds alone that occasion this slander.
Though she is tyrannous in keeping the friend from the
poet's Muse, yet she is the fairest and most precious

jewel. The poet and the friend being one, he perforce
loved what the friend loved, yet the mistresses beauty
caused a thousand groans in the poet, as she had seduced
the friend from his Muse. The 8th line denotes the
poet's absence. He is now, as in Sonnet 29, by himself
alone, and swears that though she is not fair, she is as
tyrannous as those that are, by causing in his breast the
severest pangs of love. He is still harping on the paradox
black being fair, i.e., beautiful, which is true, it being her (i.e.
Lady Rich's) deeds alone that give rise to this black slander.

Sonnet 132.—In this Sonnet the conceit of the dark
eyes being in mourning is again used. This time they
are in mourning for the poet's Muse, pitying her sorrow.
They thus appear loving mourners for the ill they have
done ; and if she will also array her heart in sorrow, even
thought it be feigned, the poet will then swear so well
does sorrow suit her that beauty is black, and there is no
beauty but that which partakes of her complexion. As
before observed, this was written at the time of the 33rd.
Shakespeare had received a missive stating them both to
be in sorrow, and as her eyes appear to mourn, so let her
heart also. He knows that her heart will not recognize
him as her real lover, her eyes but torment him ; but if her
heart will mourn also, he will then swear that all those
who are not dark like her are not beautiful.

The next and the three following Sonnets are the
counterparts of the 40th, 41st, and 42nd, addressed to
the friend, in which the friend, the mistress, and the poet
form an equilateral triangle, and bear the same loving
regard for each other. The friend loves the mistress
because the poet loves her ; and the poet loves her because

the friend loves her, and she loves the friend because the
poet loves him ; finally she loves the poet alone because
the poet and the friend are one, and that the friend may be
the Muse's love alone ; the poet offers himself as bail for
him, that he may be set free from loving servitude, and
that his own love may be accepted.

Sonnet 133.—Her heart will not love him, then ill betide
it for wounding not only himself, but his friend with him.
The poet endeavours in this and the three following
Sonnets to prove that he is alone loved by her, or at least
that she accepts his love by accepting the love of the
friend. He pleads his case as before the Court of Love :—
Ill betide that heart for the deep wound it has made
through the united hearts of both me and my friend. Is
it not enough to torture me alone ? but must my sweetest
friend be, like myself, slave to thy love (the poet having
first loved her) ; you have won both my love and his, I
am forsaken altogether (Sonnet 40, lines 9 and 10) and
bereft of all, which is a threefold torment to be thus
crossed. Take my heart prisoner in thy unrelenting
breast, but let my friend's heart be free. I will guard his
heart, thou canst not then prove a rigorous jailer, and yet
thou wilt, for if I give myself up to thee, in doing so I
give my friend's heart up also.

The poet is contented, as in the Epistle to the friend,
that she should love him ; but on condition that if
she enjoys the love of the friend, for this permission
she must accept the poet's love. His plea for desiring
to be incorporated with his friend, is that he might
guard his heart and senses. The friend, having become
enthralled by her beauty, after having devoted his

love to the poet's Muse, is the occasion to the three parties of mutual love and mutual sin ; the friend, though blamed for his fault, was at once forgiven ; but as for the lady, " her dear virtue " should have kept her from this attaint, and the poet affects that he will never forgive her for bringing this disgrace upon his Muse.

Sonnet 134.—Having confessed that the friend belongs to the mistress, the poet declares that he is mortgaged to her will, and is willing to forfeit himself if she will restore the friend to be still the consoler of his Muse ; but the mistress is too covetous to give him up, and the friend is too loving to be free. The friend has, like a surety, written for the poet under that bond that binds both poet and friend fast ; the statute of her beauty she will use and sue a friend, debtor for the poet's sake, who has lost him through her unkind abuse, and she has both the friend and poet.

The poet has lost the friend, and the mistress has them both, yet though the friend pays the whole the poet is not free. Compare this with the 42nd, in which the poet has both the mistress and the friend, yet there is no contradiction between them, it is merely looking at the same event in two different lights. If it was true to say that on account of the mutual love between the poet and his friend, they were both the poet's, it is, of course, equally true to assert that on account of their mutual love she holds them both, and thus, though the friend pays the whole debt of love, the poet is not free. In the plain matter-of-fact view too, the poet might say that he has lost the friend, since he has become estranged from him on account of the love of the mistress. Thus, she is

made against her will to claim both, and both against
their will claim her. In the 12th line of this Sonnet
there is a misprint in all the editions : " my abuse " should
be (as converted above) " thy abuse," namely, that of
taking the friend (see Sonnet 42, line 7). This Sonnet is
also in contrast to the 40th, to the friend. She is to take
all his loves, and yet merit blame for doing so. Having
chided her for making use of her beauty like a usurer his
gold, taking two for one, he now views it as her chief
grace, and entreats her still to do so.

Sonnet 135.—Runs on the trio of wills the mistress
now possesses, in which she must be happy beyond a
number, she having her own sweet will, the loving will
of the poet's friend, and the goodwill (favour and love) of
the poet himself ; so she having all, has, indeed, more
than enough. The theme is thus continued : Whoever
hath her heart's desire, thou hast thy loving will, and
will to spare, and will in abundance. I am more than
enough that still vex thee, thus making addition to thy
sweet will. Wilt thou, whose will is boundless, not once
condescend to secrete my will in thine. Shall will in
others seem right gracious, and no fair acceptance appear
in mine ? The full sea receives rain, and though boundless, still addeth to his store ; so thou, rich in will, add my
one will to increase thine. Let no fair beseecher unkindly
put me aside—think only of me and of my love.

In this Sonnet she is the pivot around which so many
mysticisms revolve, and is desired to believe that the poet
is the only one that she loves, or that loves her, that his
friend may be reserved for his Muse alone, the poet's

name being William, she may well consider him, the one she loves of that name.

Sonnet 136.—In what Butler styles " the ingenious elegancies of quibble," the poet reharps upon the punning word " Will," and ends the Sonnet attesting that it is his own christian name, as it also was the friend's. It proceeds thus : —" If thy soul should deter thee from accepting my love, thou mayst swear I was thy will, and will thou knowest is admitted there ; thus far, sweet love, thou can'st fulfil my love suit ; Will will fulfil the treasure of thy love suit, aye, fill it full of love, and my will one. In things of great receipt one is reckoned nothing, then let me in the number pass untold, though I must be one in the account ; but hold me as nought, so that thou wilt consider that nothing me, a something sweet to thee. Make but my name thy love, and then, if thou lovest that thou lovest me, for my name is Will. In the Sonnet she is desired to swear this to her " blind soul," that is, entirely give herself up to that belief.

Though widely absent, he wishes to be received in her breast as her real lover ; but this Sonnet proves that the poet had no claim whatever to the love of the lady, though he had loved her previously to the friend. The claim is merely by poetical license. A line from Troilus and Cressida may denote his former love for her, " But, though I lov'd you well, I woo'd you not." Thus, though rejected as her lover, he desires her friendship Drayton's 11th and 24th Sonnets are of a precisely similar tendency to this quartet of Shakespeare's. Drayton declares himself bewitched by his mistress ; they are so much one, that they know not themselves from each other, hence Shakespeare's parody.

Having as fruitlessly entreated her to love him as he had besought his wilful friend to marry, he, as on that occasion, changes the theme, and despairingly claims her love, the while breaking forth against himself and the mistress in the severest loving abuse. Thus, the Muse triumphs over her rival by placing her in the worst conceivable light.

Sonnet 137.—The lines in the last Sonnet

> " Among a number one is reckoned none,
> Then in the number let me pass untold."

is the occasion of the renewal of this loving abuse, which he retorts upon her for the abuse she has done him. She who has so many " saucy Jacks," probably alluding to her position at Court, must be common to all, hence she is now disdained as altogether unworthy of his love, especially as she is his greatest enemy. He begins by telling her that his eyes are like her soul blind, though not blinded by bright visions as they were for the friend ; but she is viewed as black and deformed, by reason of her evil actions, and though her eyes can rightly judge beauty, yet she, that is the best, they take to be the worst. If he knows that he but stands one among the number of her lovers, how is it that she has not only befooled his eyes, but his heart also ? Why should his heart think she is for one alone, when it knows that she is common to all the world* ; or why, his eyes seeing this, does he not say it is so ?—why seek to make the best that which

---

* Even as the sun and moon may be said to be by their pre-eminence.

is the worst. But his heart and his eyes are no true guides (alluding to his having falsely judged his true friend), and they are now turned to this false torment.

The lady is thus proved to be even as the poet's Muse guilty, yet innocent; who, though seen and admired by all, was constantly devoted to one. This begets the theme :—If she is my love, what blindness to love her, who loves another.

In the following Sonnet he continues the imaginary conversation with her, as he had done to his friend's shadow, and protests that if she will declare him her lover, he will believe himself young and her truthful.

Sonnet 138.—The theme of the last being the true and false, it is reharped upon in this. Knowing her truth, she boldly declares it, but this feigned declaration the poet converts to his own purpose. Being one with his friend, he assumes that she is alone his, and he hers ; his words are explained thus :—When his love declares that she is all truth he believes her, though he knows she speaks falsely (having seduced the friend), that she might think him some simple youth (which Herbert at that time was) for being one with the friend. The poet vainly believes that she thinks him also young, although she knows he is past the flower of his youth, and he credits her tongue, well knowing it is speaking falsely ; so on either side the simple truth is suppressed. But why does not she own that she is unjust in taking away the poet's friend ? and why does he not at once say he is old ? Because love cannot exist without trust, and the lover that is past his best does not like to count the years he has lived.

The friend being in love with the mistress, the poet must needs be also, and it is assumed for this reason that the poet and the mistress thus flatter themselves with lies.

This and the 144th Sonnet appeared in 1599 in the " Passionate Pilgrim," in the year in which they were written, and transmitted to the friend. Jaggard the printer may have obtained a copy of them from one of the " private friends." However this may be, they were careful in letting no more appear till 1609.

It appears from this Sonnet that the poet was older than the lady, as it also appears in others that the mistress was older than Herbert ; and as the poet denoted his friend's age, in the first portion of his poem, so eighteen, the number of Sonnets in this poem may denote hers ; and as the poet, for reasons given, had spoken of his being in the yellow leaf in the poem to the friend, so he again denotes it here, though he had at this date only reached his thirty-fifth year. Herbert's age was, as shown, at the date of the first Sonnets, between sixteen and seventeen, and the mistress, at the time this was written, was probably eighteen or nineteen years of age. Consequently the Muse will not view her rival as so young or so beautiful as her beloved.

Sonnet 139.—Having written pleasingly of her, it is assumed she will desire him to continue to do so, and excuse her as he had excused the friend ; but the unity is now separated, the dream is dispelled, and she is again chided for the grievous wrong she has done him and his friend, as if it caused the deepest grief. He makes this pathetic lament :—Oh ! do not look to me to make fair thy foul faults, which weigh heavily upon my heart, the taking of the friend.　See Sonnet 35, in which the poet pleads against himself to justify the wrong done to him by both the friend and the mistress.　Tell me thou lovest another (the friend), but by thy looks let me believe it to be me.　Thou needest not use art to slay me (by being silent), but when in my presence by a loving look lead me to suppose you alone love me.　You need not thus trifle with me; I should die at once at a frown. But I excuse you; it is (as in the 42nd) your love for me that induced you to love my friend.　Your pretty looks have well nigh been my death, so you kindly turn your gaze toward my friend, that he may groan under the wound of love; but do not so (he says) since I am nearly slain, kill me at once by thy loving looks.

These addresses to the visionary mistress, as those to the friend, were made in derision of the fantastical conceits used by the Italian and English sonnetteers, and these shifting changes give his satire fuller scope.　The argument of this and the foregoing Sonnet is :—Am I for thy injury to justify thy conduct, or to remain in tongue-tied patience, whilst you neither pity my state nor offer me your love?　The Muse warns either that if they continue thus to err, the crime, by being recorded allegorically, "now this ill wresting world is grown so bad," will be believed by mad ears, and then what will the mazed world think of them?　But lest this should be so, they are both bid to assent to the will of the Muse.

Sonnet 149.—The poet bids her ;—Be wise as thou art cruel; do not too much oppress me by disdaining me,

L

lest my sorrow breaks out into words, and I, wanting
pity, express my pain. If you were wise, you would
declare you love me, even if you love me not. Like im-
patient sick men when they are near their death (as he is
by the darts of her eyes) who will hear nothing from
their physicians but health, so I desire not to hear from
you the word hate, but love ; for if I despair I shall go
mad, and may speak ill of thee ; and now this ill wresting
world is grown so bad that mad slanderers are believed
by mad ears, that I may not go mad or say false things
of you, look lovingly at me alone, though thy heart loves
another. The concluding couplet resembles that of the 36th.

As she does not comply with his request, in the next
he at once becomes mad, and gives vent to his tongue-
tied patience, and thus mocks the frenzied sonnetteers.

Sonnet 141 again reverts to the theme of still loving,
though seeing every reason to hate. The poet is now
both blindly and madly in love, since he still seeks to
gain that which grieves him most ; yet in spite of his
judgment telling him that inward faults disgrace her
outward form, being united with the friend, he must
both love her and seek her love. His words may be thus
translated :—In truth, my eyes do not love thee, because
they observe a thousand errors in thee, but what they
despise my heart loves, though in all things my every
sense abhors thee. Neither in sense taste, or smell do I
desire to be invited to any feast of the senses with thee
alone (in contrast to that which he had written to the
friend, Sonnet 35, line 9), but my friend and I being one,
I cannot dissuade my foolish heart from serving thee, for

still I remain thy proud heart's wretched vassal, so that all I gain is but torment (the lady, Sonnet 42), inasmuch as the sin you occasion me to commit (*i. e.*, loving the sweet thief—see Sonnet 35) brings me but anguish (since she will neither give him her love nor give up his friend). He thus finds that he had hitherto misjudged in his com- putation of loss and gain. Our view becomes more and more evident, that it was the office of Shakespeare's Muse to praise man, as also it was her office by allegory to dis- praise woman ; hence this strikingly contrasted picture.

Sonnet 142.—The poet now expostulates with the vision of the mistress upon the sin mentioned in the last Sonnet, and it is assumed the virtuous mistress hates the sinfulness of his loving, to which he contrasts her sin ; and he denotes that as much as she loves his friend he will love her with equal right ; and as she desires the love of his friend, betrothed to his Muse, he will desire her love, trothed to his friend ; and because, though the two friends are one, she turns from him to the friend, he will protest his love for her in spite of its sin, for if he sins, she also sins ; if she seeks the friend's love he will seek hers. In the 35th, the poet has already spoken of having corrupted himself with their sins. The Sonnet is thus interpreted :—My sin is love, and you virtuously hate my sin in loving you who are another's. Oh ! but with my state compare thine own, and you shall find that it does not merit reproof, or if it does, not from thy lips that have disgraced their scarlet hue (by seducing the friend, who is married to his Muse) and sealed false bonds of love as oft as my tongue. (his pen) has forsworn itself,

robbed that which is another's (the friend belonging to
the poet's Muse) for thy own use. Is it not as lawful for
me to love thine eyes as for you to love the eyes of my
friend, whom thine woo (see Sonnet 41), as mine solicit
thee? Root pity in thy heart, that you may, when occasion serves, deserve that pity you give others; but if you
seek to have that which you hide (the friend whom she
has taken away from the poet, and who is spoken of as
lost or hid—see Sonnet 135), may you be denied the pity
you deny others. Thus they both seek to possess that
which neither have and yet both have, hence the quarrel;
and though the poet knows the mistress virtuous, he
proves her not so, since she detains, like a thief, the
friend from the Muse's garden, and prevents the flowers
of fancy springing from her beds to her beloved's honour.

Sonnet 143.—The poet now pictures this mutual
seeking to have, and allegorises this taking the poet to
her bosom, even as he had done the taking of the friend's
heart to his own breast (see Sonnet 22; it also has an
opposite reference to Sonnet 37). The mistress is now
represented as turning her eyes from the poet and pursuing the poet's other self (the friend), who is virtuously
pictured as turning from her, knowing that he is allied to
the Muse. The simile is a careful housewife (the mistress), who has lost one of her feathered creatures (Herbert), and who sets down her babe* (Shakespeare) in
order to pursue what she would have stay, not prizing

---

* She, like the Muse, pursues and desires to possess her beloved (see
Sonnet 75). The fourth, ninth, and last lines of this Sonnet (143) are in
contrast to the ninth line of Sonnet 129.

the discontent of her child, who tries to catch her. But if, having found her hope, she will turn back to him and play the mother's part by taking his love to her breast, he will then pray that she may obtain her will (*i. e.*, William, her heart's desire) and silence his loud complaining. The concluding couplet is echoed in the 136th, the idea still being—Believe me your own loving Will.[*] The reason why the friend is represented as flying from the mistress is seen in the 41st to the friend : the tempter is there shown following the youth. It is observable that he would not at first listen to her temptations, but being an untutored youth, unlearned in the world's subtleties, and the poet being absent, he had no one to advise him. The reason why the poet represents himself as her child is because she had his innocent love, seeking to be admitted into her bosom, a loving prisoner. The reader will not fail to observe the reference of the " loud crying " of this Sonnet to the " wailing chief " of the 42nd.[†]

This reharping upon the word " Will," the christian name of both the poet and the friend, is both an appropriate conclusion to his entreaty, and excuse for his love suit, and is the ending to her first epistle.

Sonnet 144.—Now all alone bereft of both her and the friend's love, the poet soliloquises his thoughts and makes an epitome of the relation between himself, the friend, and the mistress. He now places his two loves in con-

---

[*] Even the poet's contemporaries thus made this endearing use of his name, styling him " good Will." The epithet " good " is also applied to his daughter upon her epitaph, in the line—

" Wise to salvation was good Mistress Hall."

[†] The poet evidently parodies in this, the puling, whining, childish, blubbering sonneteers of his own day.

trast. The Muse has for the friend all the love of Venus for Adonis, and all the jealousy and hate for her mortal rival, which is emblematical of her sex. In the 134th, the Muse has entreated her rival to restore the friend to be her comfort. The love of the one prompts the poet like a better angel, the love of the other like an evil spirit —a woman coloured ill (spoken of as vile by the poet, not alluding to her hue, but her deeds in seducing the friend), thus causing the poet a hell of torment. (Sonnet 58) He claims two loves—the friend, whom he loves for himself, and his Muse, and the mistress, whom, in his own despite, he is compelled to love, because the friend loves her. She is again accused of tempting the friend from his side, *i.e.*, separating them, wooing him from the poet's Muse ; and converts the poet's heaven to a hell, by thus corrupting his sainted friend to be a devil, though as the poet was absent (Sonnet 41), he could not know how far she had corrupted him, but guesses each angel in the other's hell, *i.e.*, committing the same fault—the friend, adultery in loving the mistress, the mistress in loving the friend, but this the poet shall not know till the mistress relinquishes the friend. Shakespeare, while fearing that the mistress will make the friend as inconstant as herself, yet makes his Muse console herself with the thought that eventually the friend will discover that woman is faithless as the rose on her cheek, and will then perceive the full force of her (the Muse's) own truth and devotedness. The reader will at once see that this Sonnet is allied to the 67th and 68th, the doctrine there being as in this—Why should true beauty live with the false. The friend's cheek is of holy beauty, but the painted rose on woman's cheek is an impiety. Olivia, on a like loving, hating, occasion, says to her supposed Cæsario,

> " Fare thee well,
> A friend like thee might bear my soul to hell."

And Viola tells Olivia,

> " But if you were the devil, you are fair."

The expression "suggest me still" in the second line of the Sonnet, shows at once that this was not one of the first written to or of her, and is in its proper sequence. That the Sonnet was written shortly after the mystical union between the friend, is attested by this and the 138th appearing in the "Passionate Pilgrim" in 1599, and by the allusion to the same event in the early portion of the poem to the friend. It is remarkable of this and the Sonnet, above-mentioned, that they are neither addressed to the friend nor the mistress, but are self-reflections on the scheme in which the poet was then involved. They appeared in the above-mentioned miscellany the year they were written. The publisher (Jaggard) may have, as observed, obtained copies from one of the private friends, and finding they were newly written and of importance, places them first in the collection. Possibly the rest of this group of Sonnets, which were also recently written, would have been given up by the private friends, had they possessed copies. Hence it may be inferred that the Sonnets directly addressed to both the friend and the mistress respectively, were not handed about, they were merely read. This would account for no others appearing till the entire series in 1609, and with them the two printed in 1599, but revised with a few effective touches. These two Sonnets were sufficient to create a sensation, as they contained the heart of the mystery, and they evidently caused some scandal among the unknowing, some of which has reached these times, but as it rests on no foundation, it serves now as when invented, merely for jest books.

Having in this summed up the epistle addressed to the mistress, the poet has to wait till his return to know the result of her epistle of seventeen Sonnets. With this one appended, they were evidently sent with the set of seventeen to the friend, while the poet was pursuing his journey ; and he writes no more to her till his return, but he refers (as has been seen) to her influence over his other self, his friend, in the 57th 58th, and 61st Sonnets.

Upon his return, which was not till after an absence of several months, as seen in the series to the friend, after having written twenty-three Sonnets more to him while away, being the series from the 42nd to the 65th, at which point he returns, and pens the two following to the mistress. The conceit in the first arises from his having supplicated her to tell him she loved him (Sonnet 140), even though she loved him not. We find she now complies with his request, upon which the ill expressions used towards her in the last are atoned for, by the poet declaring that the spirit of evil has left her heaven and flown to hell, as the night from day.

Sonnet 145.—Is a far more cheerful self-reflection and self-flattery. The poet considers that since the mistress loves him, he should not hate her. He has returned from the journey, and to mark it he alters the stanza to the octo-syllabic ; and the lips he has chided tell him in the most loving manner that she does not hate, but loves him, for which she is indulged with a playful conceit. Being of a loving nature, she takes pity upon the poet's woful state, and, patterned by him, converts the word hate to love, and thus saves his life, (which he despaired of in absence,) by saying—I do not hate, but love you. As in the last she is proved to hate him, so now she is said to love him, which she must needs do, as he is one with the friend. Had she declared she did not love him, she would have been his hate, night, and hell, but sweet flattery, she is his love, his light, and his heaven.

Sonnet 146.— This Sonnet refers especially to Sonnets 67 and 68, belonging to the group written on the return to the friend in the most solemn strain, even so he pens her a self-reflection. The parting admonition, the farewell to the friend, is supposed to occasion in the breast of the mistress this sad lament, and this, with the last, are the only lines addressed to her on his return. Thus the poet treated her in the same manner as the friend, whom, however, the Muse indulged with thirteen Sonnets, though she can spare but two for the mistress. It is to be observed in renewing the song he translated the " coloured ill " of the 144th to " false of hue," to give wider scope to the satire. This is, indeed, a noble Sonnet. It attests the poet's faith in the immortality of the soul ; and shows that he thought, as he elsewhere expresses it, " nobly of the soul." In this Sonnet we view the poet reading a homily to the mistress, upon the vanity of earthly things ; and as the end of the poem is now contemplated, she is warned of of her end, and besought to defy death and live for ever ; but it is not to be by verse, but by despising outward vanities, *i.e.*, painting and cost, and to rather seek divine love, which exists beyond the grave. This, like the rest, though addressed to her, alludes directly to the women of the age, for had she been a painted woman, she would have been loathed, rather than loved by two such sensitive upholders of nature's own painting, and detesters of all artificial aids to beauty. She is besought to let her mind banquet though her body pine, and bid her soul adorn itself with divine graces, to gain an eternal life ; and not be the despised servant of the body, but its master, since all painting and cost soon become food for worms.*

RENEWAL.

The poet renews the complaint, and the following eight Sonnets are evidently written during the time of the renewal of the song to the friend, between Sonnets 77 and 126 ; and as the poet had told his friend that his love still continued for him, so he tells the mistress (that in spite of the Muse's allegorical dislike to her), he still continues to love her, and that he has been love-sick for her, his food having been his loving thoughts. It is worthy of remark in these last Sonnets and their counterparts to the friend, that the allegory is further developed, for the purpose of a more direct satire upon the marriages a-la-mode of the age. He also ceases to speak of the friend, but vainly supposes the friend and himself are one, and that she loves him only ; for the same reason in the counterpart renewal to the friend, Sonnets 77 to 126, no mention is made of her.

---

* In the second line of the Sonnet there is a misprint, the words "my sinful earth" are repeated, instead of, I conjecture, "Poor soul ;" the line will then stand thus, "Poor soul, those rebel powers that thee array."

Sonnet 147.—Returning to the former theme of his impure love for the sweet thief, he now likens his love to a fever, and he has a sickly appetite, for that which increases it, and he holds this weak state, bordering upon insanity, to be an additional reason why she should give up the friend ; and yet, as in Sonnet 118, he would not lose the love, of whose sweetness he is so sick. In the height of his delirium he cries, I have sworn thee fair and thought thee radiant, when thou art black as hell, and dark as night, alluding to the praise he had given her during the interim of silence, when he had supposed she was his alone, by her sweet flattery, Sonnet 145.

As in the last, he pictures her fair without but foul within, merely outside show, because she refuses to give up the friend married to the Muse ; nevertheless his love exceeded during absence what it was before ; and as in the last he speaks of life, its support, and death, so now he renews the song by speaking of love, its support, and death.

Sonnet 148.—Love reasons without reason is again the theme ; and, as in the last, he still affirms his judgment has left him. Harping upon the concluding lines of the last Sonnet, he continues upbraiding love :—O me ! what eyes has love given me, which bear no resemblance to true seeing eyes, or if they do, my judgment has left me, since they estimate falsely that which they see truly ! If that be fair on which my false eyes love to dwell, why do others say it is not so ? (reverting to the paradox of black being fair). If it be not, then the eye of love observes truly. But love's eye cannot be true, it is so obscured by watching (lest she should take the friend entirely), and

in tears (for his having proved guilty), that it is no
wonder that I do not see clearly; the sun itself sees
not till heaven clears. He concludes that she purposely
keeps him blind, lest he should discover her treacherous
faults (the seducing the friend from Shakespeare's Muse).
That the friend is not now recognised is imputed to her
cunning love keeping the poet blind.

Sonnet 149.—The mistress, like the friend (Sonnet
102) thinks that on account of the poet having ceased
the mystic song addressed to her, he has ceased loving;
but how can he cease to love her, or she him, while she
loves Herbert, and he her? Can she say that the poet does
not love her, when he arms himself in her cause, and thus
for her sake plays the tyrant to himself, just as he had for
the friend, and proves himself her slave in all loving submissiveness? He exclaims :—Would I call any my
friend who does not love you, or whom you do not love?
and if you frown upon me, am I not at once full of
grief?—or, in other words, if he is hated by her he will
hate himself. He asks what worthiness he values in
himself that should make him so proud as to despise
being her servant, while all his best, obedient to the
command of her eye, worships her fault, and convert it to
her best grace. As in the 92nd he tells his friend that if
he ever ceases loving he will not observe it, so he now
tells her that though he observes she loves another, he will
be blind, and not see it. The quibbling is at once
evident upon the sounds of the words eye and I. As
before observed, the language to both the friend and the
mistress on the renewal is of a like tendency. Compare
also with this Sonnets 89 and 120.

Sonnet 150.—Though the poet has seen and heard more of her faults (during the interim), yet he now loves her more. He is thus led to ask whence the mistress has gained this powerful might, so as to make him palliate all her worst deeds and belie his own vision. How is it he converts her worst of all worsts to the best of all bests? (by taking the friend from the Muse, by which she gives a triumphant proof of her skill in the art and mystery of love). Who taught him to love the more the more cause he saw for hate? (in her seeking to possess the friend); and though he loves what others hate (a divider and corrupter of loving friends), she should not abhor his despised state. However unworthy his love may be, it should be received, since her unworthiness has raised love in him, he is the more worthy to be loved by her. This Sonnet not only refers to the same event, but is a renewed counterpart of Sonnets 40 and 93. It is perceivable that under the mask of allegory the mistress was to translate this loving abuse to her praise.

Sonnet 151.—This was evidently written about the time of the 115th. The poet's love for her is a growing love, and his soul tells him she is alone his own. In this and the following Sonnet, which ends the loving war, it is decided that both are in fault, but the poet mostly so, and he finally pays her the highest compliment the argument admits of, when he says in the following Sonnet—

> "But why of two oaths' breach do I accuse thee,
> When I break twenty?" (I am perjured most).

Having spoken of her soul's sin being outward show, he now declares it to be also love, and discourses upon his soul's sin (love) ; at the same time, stating that his soul is master of his " gross body," not, as was the case with the mistress, the body triumphing over the soul. He makes apology for the loving fault of her unworthiness raising love in him, but he does not accuse himself for this sinful loving of a want of conscience. He thus justifies it :— Love is too young to know what conscience is, yet conscience may be the offspring of love. She is not, then, to urge the poet's fault in loving her, when she is equally guilty in loving the friend. They are thus both guilty of the same fault ; but since she has acted treacherously to him, he will act so to her. He will direct towards her his full soul of love (which he may do in the name of his friend, as they are but one), and having, by this union with the friend, both the friend and the mistress, he may well triumph in love, and stay no further examination of conscience, and though she is the love of the friend, he may point her out as his triumphant prize. Having gained so much, he is contented to be her vassal, and to rise and fall in her love and hate as she purposes, for he counts it no want of conscience to seek her love, even though she may refuse to give it ; and since he and his friend are one, she is unquestionably the poet's own dear mistress. Thus the poet offers himself, both body and soul, as her devoted servant, to be loved or hated as she chooses, and he bids her tell her soul, as in the 136th, to deceive itself, and love but him alone. This Sonnet is the very counterpart of the 124th to the friend ; it also has a covert allusion to Antony Scoloker's* " Diaphantus ;

* Scoloker may however have seen this Sonnet of Shakespeare's, they appear to have been friends, and he styles him " friendly Shakespeare."

or the Passions of Love," edit. 1604, stanza 2. The conceit of the Sonnet itself arose in the concluding couplet of the last; but, as observed, it stands in contrast to the erection of loving verse to the friend, Sonnets123, 124.

Sonnet 152.—He continues his own betrayal, and urges hers. The mistress having said she also loves the poet, they are thus mutually in fault, both have now newly protested love (she in the 145th, he in the 149th). He lovingly rebukes her, and as in the 36th and 117th he flings the greatest disgrace upon himself, so he does with equal truth upon the present occasion. He exclaims:— Thou knowest that in loving thee I am forsworn (having promised to love only the friend), but thou art twice forsworn, to me, love swearing (the two friends being but one, she has protested her love for the poet alone, yet given it to the friend); he demands why he accuses her of breaking two oaths, when he breaks twenty. He is perjured most, since all he has said in her praise in the interim of peaceful love proves to her dispraise, and all the honest faith he had in her is gone; for he has sworn she was not unloving, inconstant, or ill-coloured, and to give her brightness he gave light to his own blindness, or made his eyes swear against the object of their vision. Because (he says) I have sworn thee fair (Sonnet 127) I am most perjured to swear in the face of truth so foul a lie.* She is then proved both false without and within, and the aim and end of the satire fulfilled; and as in the 35th the poet excused his friend's sins more than his sins were, so the

---

* He thus finally protests that she was not fairer than the fair, but blacker than the black.

sins of the mistress are blamed more than her sins were ;
and as she deserves the severest indignation of the poet's
Muse, she is not to be entirely forgiven. She has now
received her final denunciation, which, however, bears
love in itself. In the two concluding Sonnets the poet
pleads that his having left her arose from excess of love,
which was also the plea he made to the friend for leaving
him ; and as on his return and renewal of the Sonnets his
love for the friend had increased, so also his love for the mistress must needs have increased. So now we have witnessed
that the poet's computation of loss and gain, summed up in
Sonnet 42, was in vain, for the mistress has won the friend
from the Muse, and the poet has not gained her love,
though the Muse despairingly claimed the friend, and the
poet the mistress, and the friend and mistress each other.
As the poet began Sonnet 127 by praising her mourning eyes, and claiming her as his own, he now ends with
the like claim and the like praise.

Sonnet 153.—The poet ends the series with an allusion
to Cupid, and offers the highest praise to the mistress.
This was evidently written about the time of the 118th and
119th to the friend ; and the poet, as observed, now excuses
his having left the mistress on account of his seeking a cure
for his mad loving. In this and the following Sonnet
he sports with a conceit in which he refers to his
present mad state and to the absence of the past ; and as
he has told the friend in the above denoted Sonnets that
he left him being replete with his sweet love, and
" sickened to shun sickness," in like manner he excused
his absence to the mistress, and left her to get cured of

his mad loving fever.* In doing this, he relates a poetic origin of the Bath waters. He is led to do so by assuming that he sought these waters as a cure for his "strange malady," i. e., excess of love. So hither he hied, "a sad, distempered guest." But at these efficacious waters he "found no cure." The only bath, he flatters her, that would cure him is her tearful eyes.

It is worthy of remark that though the city of Bath is not directly named, the allusions may be to it, as the most famous of waters. The Romans termed them "the waters of the sun," and there erected altars to Diana. But from the following, Shakespeare may equally allude to the wells of Buxton.

J. Jones dedicated his "Bathes of Bathes Ayde" to Henry, Earl of Pembroke. This work Shakespeare appears to have perused. The author enters into a long discussion upon the properties of the waters and the cause of their heat. Upon the latter subject no definite conclusion is arrived at. In his description he uses the term "valley fountains." Jones further says, "The well springs be situated in a valley, hard by a running brook." This Sonnet denotes the same situation. He adds "and those very excellent and beneficial for divers distemperatures, griefs, and sicknesses." Bath is also referred to by numerous contemporary writers as being a place of fashionable resort. He makes allusion to Cupid on account of the mystery of his own enduring love, thus imputing the blame of his loving to the god of love ; the bath being heated by the torch of love, has added love to

---

† This grows out of the 147th ; his reason left him, and he without reason left her.

M

his already love inflamed heart, the trial upon his heart having proved far too effectual.

Sonnet 154.—This is a variation of the last,* and possibly the last Sonnet that Shakespeare ever wrote ; and, like Cupid, who laid by his brand, he laid by his pen—the pen of love. The argument ends by the poet claiming the mistress as his own, and protesting his love for her without mentioning the friend, even as the poem to the friend ends by his claiming him without mention of the mistress. He has now ended his poem as he commenced it, by extolling her mournfulness, and her lover's only cure for his complaint is, that he may be submerged in her tearful eyes, a bath which also increases his love for her, on account of her sorrow for her fault ; and though his Muse will not forgive her, he does so, and will claim her love.

Thus, by the magic of verse, the poet has celebrated the mystical marriage of his Muse, and drawn all love to himself ; defied time, and that iconoclast death, the destroyer of living images ; erected a time-defying monument to his friend, and rendered himself immortal ; and though the friend was permitted to become forgotten, partly owing to the poet dying within seven years of the publication of these poems, but more especially by the poet's glory becoming a few years later eclipsed by the cloud of envious rivalry, insomuch, that we are told by a poet of the period, that

> " Shakespeare no glory was allowed,
>   His sun quite sunk beneath a cloud,"

---

* In the first the relation is equally divided, this is chiefly concerning the cold fruitless votary of Diana. This singular repetition may also mark a distinctive ending.

referring to the works of Jonson and Beaumont and
Fletcher taking the place of Shakespeare's; and as the
mystical Sonnets were understood but by a few during
the life-time of the friends, and less so after their deaths,
and as the poet's sun had set, though in glory, to rise
again with still greater splendour, yet, consequent upon
this setting, a shade was cast over his memory, and his
Sonnets were permitted to sink into oblivion, though both
the poet and the patron, and other far-seers foresaw, that
though the age in which they lived slighted the mystic
memorial of their friendship, that the time would come
when both poet and patron would receive by the Sonnets
both honour and glory.

That the friend would live in them the poet was
assured, on account of the description given of him and
his initials in the dedication, even if the allusions to the
rival poets did not discover him; and on the part of the
patron, by his having the poet's collected plays dedicated
to him, seven years after the poet's death, as the work of his
servant Shakespeare, whom he had prosecuted while living
with so much favour, which at once connects him with
the Sonnets as the poet's exalted patron and loving friend.
And was not the marriage of Herbert to the Muse a theme
worthy of our great poet, apart from the sacred wedlock
of friendship, which rite and ceremony, the most lovely
and most loving Muse has so divinely and exquisitely
celebrated.

Thus the whole of this confession of sins, the crimes,
stains, and blots, prove, when divested of allegory, in the
words by which the Comedy is known, in which Herbert
is personified, to be but "Much Ado about Nothing;"

but the object of both the patron and the poet was accomplished in this satire upon mistress sonnetting, and to one poet's mistress evidently especial allusion is made, for whoever will glance at the life of the lady Rich, the Stella whom Sidney sonnetted so divinely, will discover that she was just such a woman as is here described. King James designated her " a fair woman, with a black soul." At this famous frail married woman, Shakespeare, in all probability, chiefly levels his allegorical satire.* Who the lady was our poet addressed I have not been able to discover, but from various hints I conjecture she was a star of the Court of Elizabeth, whom Shakespeare admired for her wit and beauty ; and upon Herbert becoming her lover, as shown, it was arranged between them, Shakespeare should picture allegorically their love as a satire upon mistress sonnetting, probably out of spite to the lady Rich, both upon the part of the lady whom Herbert loved,† and upon the young lord's, who may have had some family reason for this, for we know not what offence this scandalous woman

---

* It is recorded that in the years 1599-1600, Lady Rich was more closely attached to Mountjoy than to her husband. Herbert's aversion to marriage might have arisen from the example he had witnessed in Sidney's mistress ; she presented a totally opposite picture to Herbert, to that which she had some years previously to Sidney, both as regards her beauty and virtues. Herbert being a melancholy young man, devoted more to the Muses than Mistresses, upon his becoming a friend of Shakespeare, at once fell in with his notions of the absurdity of the Sonneteers, each extolling the object of his own choice as the most beautiful though she were the most deformed, as supremely virtuous though she were extremely immoral, and each loudly proclaiming the immortality of their goddesses ; seeing this Herbert instigated Shakespeare, who readily complied, to make sport of them, and desired him to direct the allusions chiefly to Lady Rich, the Stella of Sidney's song. The reader has seen how Shakespeare effected this, and how Herbert suggested and delighted in the satire.

† She must unquestionably have been as great a wit, as volatile, and as strong minded as Beatrice.

gave to the Pembrokes, through the dishonour she brought upon her sex, upon the Court, and upon the noble Sidney, he having prostituted his pen in sonnetting her.

I find mention of her as the evil angel of Sidney in the poems of Ann Bradstreet, the daughter of T. Dudley, Esq. She wrote some of her poems in America, and is styled the tenth Muse, lately sprung up there. In her Elegy upon Sir Philip Sidney, written in 1638, she severely censures that blazing star of the Elizabethian constellation as having been of ill omen.

After a long panegyric upon Sidney, she says of "illustrious Stella"—

> "I fear thou wert a comet, did portend,
> Such prince as he, his race should shortly end;
> If such stars as these, such presagers be,
> I wish no more such blazes we may see ;!
> But thou art gone, such meteors never last,
> And as thy beauty, so thy name would waste ;
> But that it is record by Philip's hand,
> That such an omen once was in our land."

Our poetess does not omit to state that however adulterate others, love may have been, his was pure. She concludes with an eulogy on Sidney, and ends the elegy with these lines—

> "So Sidney's fame I leave to England's rolls,
> His bones do lie interr'd in stately Pauls."

ADDITIONAL NOTES

TO THE DOUBLE POEM, CONSISTING OF ONE HUNDRED AND TWENTY-SIX SONNETS.

The following notes are extracted from a large series which I had collected to illustrate every Sonnet. I have inserted only those I thought of most interest to general readers, as illustrating the theme.

The booksellers who were to sell Shakespeare's Sonnets had their names and addresses placed at the bottom of the title-page. Eld printed them, Aspley and Wright sold them, and Thorpe paid the expenses of typography. W. Aspley, in 1623, was one of the four printers of the first folio.

THE DEDICATION.

"Shakespeare's Sonnets, author's edition, with an inscriptional dedication, at Althorpe, in Lord Spenser's library, is a very fine copy, inscribed "To my very kind friend," which may or may not be a presentation copy from Shakespeare himself."—*Lowndes' Biblio. Man.*, 1863.

"Begetare : as a father, genitor."—*Promptorium Parvulorum.*

"Like the father that begets them."—1 *Henry IV.*

The title-page of the second edition runs thus :—
" Poems written by Wil. Shakespeare, Gent., London : by T. Cotes for John Benson, 1640." Thos. Cotes, in 1632, was the printer of the second folio for Robert Allot. Every right leaf of the volume has " Shakespeare's " name at the top, and every left, the word " Sonnets."

SONNET 1.

Line 1.

" Dau. No, faith ! how mean you with encrease, Sir John !

Daw. Why, with encrease is when I court her for the common cause of mankind.

Daw. Then this is a ballad of procreation.

Cleir. A madrigal of procreation ; you mistake."—*Jonson's Epicœne.*

Line 2.

" The rose and expectancy of the fair state."—*Hamlet.*

SONNET 2.

Line 1.

" These forty winters have I married been."—*Sidney's Arcadia.*

Lines 10, 11, 12.

" Looking on the lines
Of my boy's face, methought I did recoil
Twenty-three years."—*Winter's Tale.*

SONNET 4.

Lines 3, 4.

" Nature never lends
The smallest scruple of her excellence,
But, like a thrifty goddess, she determines
Herself the glory of a creditor,
Both thanks and use."—*Measure for Measure.*

Lines 7, 8.

" Beauty is nature's coin ; must not be hoarded,
But must be current."—*Comus.*

SONNET 5.

Lines 9 *to* 14.

" But earthlier happy is the rose distilled
Than that which, withering on the virgin thorn,
Grows, lives, and dies in single blessedness."
Midsummer Night's Dream.

Line 14.

" Leese " is an old word for loose. Dogberry, stumbling over this word when he intends to say " leases," stupidly says " leeses." The joke is spoilt by being printed " losses", he was an householder.

SONNET 7.

Lines 1 *to* 6.

" Eros, turn from me, then, that noble countenance
Wherein the worship of the whole world lies."
Antony and Cleopatra.

Lines 12, 13.

"Men shut their doors against a setting sun."—*Timon of Athens.*

SONNET 8.

Lines 1 to 4.

"I can sing
And speak to him in many sorts of music,
That will allow me, very worth his service."—*Twelfth Night.*

"It is the tune surely of Sonnets, they are all the choice ;
Poets do keep them as a charming thing."

Scoloker's Diaphantas, 1604.

Lines 1 to 10.

"My untuned, stringed verse do thou excuse."

R. Chester's Love's Martyr, 1601.

Lines 12 and 13.

"Better music ne'er was known
Than a quire of hearts in one."

Beaumont's Knight of the Burning Pestle.

SONNET 9.

Lines 13 and 14.

"Immortal be preserved,
If thus thou murder thy posterity ;
Thy very being thou hast not deserved."—*Sidney's Arcadia.*

SONNET 10.

Lines 1 to 4.

"The young courtier William Herbert is exceedingly beloved of all men"—"he greatly wants advice." Again, "My lord Herbert is very well. I don't find any disposition at all in this gallant young Lord to marry." "He is also very well beloved here of all, especially by 200 and 40 who protest in all places they love him." "My Lord Herbert is not come up according to his appointment, and writes unto me ; but if it be possible he will be here before Christmas or New Year's day. There passes most kind letters between him and 40 such, as are shown to 1500 (the Queen), and I find 40 most willing to do him any service."

Extracts from Letters of Robert White to Sir Robert Sydney, 1599.

"It is certain I am loved of all ladies, only you excepted ; and I would I could find it in my heart, that I had not a hard heart, for truly I love none."

"The world must be peopled. When I said I would die a bachelor, I did not think that I should live till I were married."

Much Ado about Nothing.

Lines 7, 8.

"O sister seek within thyself to flourish,
Thy house by thee must live or else be gone."

Sidney's Arcadia.

SONNET 11.

Line 1.

" I grow and wither both together."—*George Whither, ætat* 21, 1611.

Lines 7, 8.

" But this I am sure, quoth Coridon, if all maidens were of her mind, the world would grow to a mad fray, for then would be such store of wooing and little wedding."—*Lodge's Rosalynde.*

Lines 9, 10.

"Sir, I know you not, but that you live an injury to nature."
Fletcher's Pilgrim.

Lines 13, 14.

" Yet, put it by, lest thou dear Lord, Narcissus
Like, should dote upon thyself, and die, and rob
The world of nature's copy, that she works
Forms by."—*Massinger's Fatal Dowry.*

SONNET 13.

Lines 1, 2

"Thou art not thyself,
For thou existed on many a thousand grains,
That issue out of dust."—*Measure for Measure.*

SONNET 15.

Line 3.

"All the world's a stage,
And all the men and women merely players."—*As You Like it.*

Lines 3, 4.

" But, O you powers
That give heaven countless eyes to view men's acts."—*Pericles.*

Line 11.

"Nature and sickness
Debate it at their leisure."—*All's Well that Ends Well.*

Line 12.

" Hath dimmed your infant morn to aged night."—*King Richard III.*

SONNET 16.

Line 9.

" For though his line of life went soon about,
The life yet of his lines shall never out."
Hugh Holland on Shakespeare.

Line 14.
" With his sweet skill my skilless youth he drew."—*Sidney's Arcadia.*

SONNET 17.
Lines 1 *to* 12.
" Some misbelieving and profane in love,
    When I do speak of miracles by thee,
May say thou art flattered by me."—*Drayton's Sonnets.*

SONNET 18.
Lines 1 *and* 2.
" And she is fair too, is she not,
    As a fair day in summer, wondrous fair."—*Pericles.*

SONNET 19.
Line 14.
" If there may be a perpetual youth bestowed on man, I am that soul
shall win it.—*Fletcher's Queen of Corinth.*

SONNET 20.
Line 1.
" A youth so sweet of face,
That many thought him of the female race."—*Marlowe.*
Line 2.
"Our general himself makes a mistress of him—our general is cut i'
the middle, and but one half of what he was yesterday, for the other has
half, by the entreaty and grant of the whole table."—*Coriolanus.*

ALMANZ.   The man who dares like you in fields appear,
            And meet my sword shall be my mistress here.
D'ARCOS.   I shall be glad by which ere means I can,
            To get the friendship of so brave a man."—*Dryden.*
Line 7.
" Nevertheless, however, they are restrained to their several similitudes,
it is certain that all of them desire no form or figure so much as the likeness
of a man, and do think themselves in heaven, when they are infeast in that
hue."—*Of the Naids and Nereides, Nash's Pierce Penniless.*
      " But if in living colours and bright hue,
        Thyself thou covet to see pictured.
        Who can do it ?—lively or more true,
        Than that sweet verse with nectar sprinkled.."—*Fairy Queen.*
Line 10.
          " For still
    Nature did dote on him (her Bellamour
    Or masterpiece) the wonder of her skill."
The Muse's Tears for Henry, Prince of Wales, J. Davies, 1613.

SONNET 21.

Line 1.

Fletcher in the following passage in the "Woman Hater" (1608) has an allusion to the mistress-sonnetteers. Gondarius exclaims—" The women of this age (if there be any degree of comparison amongst their sex) are worse than those of former times, for I have read of women of that truth and constancy, that were they now living, I would endure to see them ; but I fear the writers of the time belied them, for how familiar a thing is it with the poets of our age to extol their whores (which they call mistresses) with heavenly praises ; but I thank their furies and crazed brains beyond belief. Nay, how many that would fain seem serious, have dedicated works to ladies toothless, hollow-eyed, their hair shedding, purple faced, their nails apparently coming off, and the bridges of their noses broken down, and have called them the choice handy words of nature, the patterns of perfection, and the wonderment of women." It will be seen from this alone the opinion the wits of the day would have upon Shakepeare's Sonnets to his friend ; they could well participate in the poet's object.

Line 1.

I have discovered that the lady whom Drayton addressed bore the initials L. S. (query, a Sidney ?). I gain my knowledge of this from the circumstance, that among the Dedicatory Poems by Drayton, which are prefixed to his collected works in Chalmer's collection, one is thus headed :—" To the lady L. S.," beginning with the words, " Bright star of beauty." In the " Ideas " it stands the 4th. There are many improvements in the one so titled.

Line 2.

" Women who do paint themselves to seem beautiful do clean deface the image of their Creator."—*Mere's Wit's Commonwealth,* 1598.

Line 2.

"Though thou rentest thy face with painting, in vain shalt thou make thyself fair ; thy lovers will despise thee."—*Jeremiah.*

The 9th line of this Sonnet contains the poet's motto, " True in Love." His seal, preserved at Stratford, bears the initials " W. S," entwined with the true lovers' knot.

Lines 13, 14.

" We'll not commend what we intend not to sell."—*Troilus and Cressida.*

SONNET 22.

Line 4.

" Make haste, the hour of death is expiate."—*Richard III.*

Lines 5 to 12.

" His heart in me keeps me, and him in me ;
My heart in him his thoughts and senses guide ;
He loves my heart, for once it was his own ;
I'll cherish his because in me it bides."—*Sir P. Sidney.*

Lines 11 to 14.

" My heart I gave thee, not to do it pain,
But to preserve it to thee was taken.
I served thee, not that I should be forsaken,
But that I should receive reward again."—*Sir T. Wyatt,* 1552.

SONNET 23.

Lines 1 to 4.

" Like a dull actor, now
" I have forgat my part, and I am out,
Even to a full disgrace."—*Coriolanus.*

Line 4.

" Weakens you are, dare you with your strength fight,
Because your weakness weakens all your might ?"
Sidney's Arcadia.

Lines 5 to 9.

" My lord will go away to-night ;
A very serious business calls on him,
The prerogative and rite of love,
Which, as your due time claims, he doth acknowledge,
But puts it off by a compelled restraint."
All's Well that Ends Well.

Line 12.

" My tongue is the pen of a reader writer."—*Psalms.*

Lines 9 to 14.

" My looks shall be love, and wit's record-books,
  Wherein she still may read what I conceive
  Of her sweet words, and what replies I give."

Sonnet by J. Davies.

SONNET 24.

Lines 1 to 12.

" Love in my heart thy heavenly shape doth paint;
  Thine eye the glass wherein I behold my heart,
  Thine eye the window through the which mine eye
  May see my heart, and thee thyself espy."—*Constable's Diana.*

SONNET 25.

Line 4.

" Love sought is good, but given unsought is better."—*Twelfth Night.*

Lines 5 to 8.

The lowly flower we call the marigold is not that which Shakespeare meant. The flower he describes is the sunflower, which was formerly called the Mary Gold. So in Greene's " Farewell to Folly:"—" The nature of this herb, Lady Frances, which we call the Mary Gold, is called by the Latinists Sol Sequiam."

" O you, thrice famoused for rarity !"—*N. Deeble on John Davies*, 1603.

SONNET 28.

Line 1.

" A labour'd line is too busy for my brain,
  That is well nigh distracted with much thought."

Sonnet by J. Davies.

Line 9.

" Thou standest in the rising sun,
  And in the setting thou art fair."—*In Memoriam.*

Line 12.

" I saw the wench that twirred and twinkled at thee."

Fletcher—Women Pleased.

Belarius (of the princes) :—

> " They are worthy
> To inlay heaven with stars."—*Cymbeline*.

SONNET 29.

Lines 1, 2.

" You do surely but bar the door upon your own liberty if you deny your griefs to your friend."—*Hamlet.*

Line 3.

" Witness my throat made hoarse with thundering cries."

> *Sonnet in Poetical Rhapsody*, 1602.

SONNET 30.

Line 1.

" I and my bosom must debate awhile,
And then I would no other company."—*Henry V.*

Line 3.

" You draw my spirits from me
With new lamenting ancient oversights."

> *Henry IV.*, *Part* 2.

Line 8.

> " And cursed man
> Shall ne'er more renew his vanished face."

> *Byron's Tragedy by Chapman*, 1608.

Line 12.

" Which I will be ever to pay, and yet pay still."—*Cymbeline.*

SONNET 31.

Lines 9, 10.

" Since I their altar, you empatron me."—*Lover's Complaint.*

Lines 13, 14.

" True and perfect friendship is to make one heart and mind of many hearts and bodies."—*Mere's Wit's Commonwealth.*

SONNET 32.

Lines 1, 2.

" Be absolute for life or death ; either death or life
Shall thereby be the sweeter."—*Measure for Measure.*

Line 4.

" It is the witness still of excellency
To put a strange face on his own perfection."

> *All's Well that Ends Well.*

Lines 4, 5, 13, 14.

'But weak and lowly are these tun'd lays,
If for such favour they have worthless striven :
Since love their cause was, be that love forgiven."
Dedication by W. Brown to Lord Pembroke.

Line 14.

"No style is held for base where love well named is."—*Sidney's Arcadia.*

SONNET 33.

Lines 1 to 14.

"But in this clear and brightsome day
I see a black suspicious cloud appear
That will encounter with our glorious sun ;
I mean those powers which the queen hath got in France
Are landed, and mean once more to menace us."
Second Part of the original King Henry the Sixth.

Line 12.

"Behold the clouds which have eclipsed my sun."—*Drayton.*

Line 12.

"Clouds, when they intercept our sight,
Deprive us of celestial light ;
Let me proclaim it then aloud
That every woman is a cloud."—*Swift.*

SONNET 34.

Lines 1, 2.

"Eke Romeus, when he saw his long desyred sight,
His mourning cloke of mone put off." - *Old Poem.*

Line 3.

"In my way": *query,* "on my way."

Line 6.

"Witness the showers which still fall from mine eyes,
And breast with sighs like stormy winds near rived."
Sonnet in Poetical Rhapsody, 1602.

Lines 1 to 14.

"Alas ! my lord, it is your shine must comfort us.
Alas ! I shine in tears like the sun in April."—*Tourneir.*

SONNET 35.

Line 9.

"Receive the incense which I offer here."—*Drayton, Sonnet 54.*

Lines 9 to 14.

"THEOD. What ! my Varannes, will you be so cruel
As not to see my bride before you go ?
Or are you angry at your rival's charms,
Who has already ravished half my heart,
Which once was all your own ?"—*Lee's Theodosius.*

SONNET 36.

Lines 1 to 4.

"My stars shine darkly over me; the malignity of my fate might perhaps distemper yours; therefore I shall crave of you your leave that I may bear my evils alone; it were a sad recompense to lay any of them on you."—*Twelfth Night.*

Lines 11, 12.

The Earl of Pembroke was well reputed for being constant in his patronage and friendship, not weighing differences of state. Among the poems of George Whithers, of which there were two editions, there is an epigram to William Earl of Pembroke. The first edition, 1611, has a line which stands thus :—

"Thou whom respect of kin makes not unjust."

In the edition of 1613, it is altered to :—

"Thou whom no private ends can make unjust."

Dr. Chalmers has shown that, as Lord Chamberlain, he endeavoured, upon the publication of Shakespeare's plays, seven years after the death of the poet, to protect his writings from surreptitious publication, and tried to transmit the poet's fame to eternal date. Thus Shakespeare had no real cause to fear he would desert him.

SONNET 37.

Line 4.

"You have confirmed me. Who would love a woman
That might enjoy in such a man a friend ?"
Massinger's Fatal Dowry.

Line 7.

"Cæsar's better parts
Shall be crowned in Brutus."—*Julius Cæsar.*

SONNET 39.

Lines 1 to 4.

"Friendship ought to resemble the love between man and wife—that is, two bodies to be made one will and affection."—*Meré's Wit's Commonwealth.*

Lines 1 to 4.

" Sith God, and king, and your mind's sympathy,
Hath made you two an undivided one."

John Davies to Lord Ph. Herbert and
Sir James Haies, Knt.

" To praise thee, being what I am to thee,
Were (in effect) to dispraise thee and me ;
For who doth praise himself deserves dispraise ;
Thou art myself, then thee I may not praise."

R. Davies to his brother, John Davies.

Lines 13, 14.

" Our separation so abides and flies
That thou, residing here, go'st yet with me,
And I, hence fleeting, yet remain with thee."

Antony and Cleopatra.

Lines 13, 14.

" To a Friend.

" What though our absent hands may not enfold
Real embraces, yet we firmly hold
Each other in possession."—*Sonnet by Lord Pembroke.*

SONNET 40.

Line 1.

" My love without retention, or restraint,
All his in dedication."—*Twelfth Night.*

Lines 1 to 10.

" Either was the other's mine."

" Property was thus appalled
That the self was not the same."

Shakespeare, The Phœnix and Turtle, 1601.

SONNET 42.

Lines 1 to 12.

" Her love to both,
And each to other, and all loves to both,
Draw after her ; pardon what I have spoke,
For 'tis a studied, not a present thought,
By duty ruminated."—*Antony and Cleopatra.*

Lines 1 to 14.

" Oli.   'Twas never merry world,
Since lowly feigning was call'd compliment.
You are servant to the Count Orsino, youth ?
Viol. And he is yours, and his must needs be yours ;
Your servant's servant is your servant, madam."

Twelfth Night.

SONNET 44.

Lines 13, 14.

" Distempered messengers of wit,
Badges of bitterness."—*Much Ado about Nothing.*

SONNET 45.

Lines 1 to 12.

" Love is, and was, my lord and king,
And in his presence I attend,
To hear the tidings of my friend,
Which every hour his couriers bring."—*In Memoriam.*

SONNET 46.

Lines 5 to 12.

" The matter is grown to an issue ; there must be a jury impanelled, and
I would desire and entreat you to be one of the guests."—*Greene's Quip for
an Upstart Courtier,* 1597.

Lines 5 to 14.

" My eyes should surfeit by my heart's content."
Lines prefatory to Greene's Arcadia, 1589.

SONNET 48.

Line 8.

" The rising sun night's vulgar lights destroys."—*Waller.*

Line 14.

" Rich preys make true men thieves."—*Venus and Adonis.*

SONNET 49.

Line 14.

" For he himself is subject to his birth."—*Hamlet.*

SONNET 51.

Lines 1 to 8.

" Imo. O for a horse with wings."—*Cymbeline.*

SONNET 52.

Line 8.

" But her hand my muse captain holds."—*Davies' Sonnets.*

SONNET 53.

Lines 1 to 6.

> "I will think thy pictures be
> (Image like of saints' perfection) poorly counterfeiting thee."
>
> *Sir P. Sidney's Sonnets.*

Line 8.

"And antique praises unto present persons fit."—*Fairy Queen.*

"His native hue is a lily white,
Youthful and blithe, if suited in a rosy tire."—*Phineas Fletcher.*

SONNET 54.

This Sonnet has been imitated by Henry Peacham in the "Minerva Britannia," 1612, p. 100.

SONNET 55.

"CONCERNING THE HONOUR OF BOOKS.

> "Since honour from the honourer proceeds,
> How well do they deserve that memory
> And leave in books for all posterities
> The names of worthies, and their vertuous deeds
> When all their glory else, like water weeds
> Without their element, presently dies,
> And all their greatness quite forgotten lies ;
> And when, and how they flourish't no man heeds.
> How poor remembrances, are statues, tombs,
> And other monuments that men erect
> To Princes, which remain in closed rooms
> Where but a few behold them ; in respect
> Of books, that to the universal eye
> Show how they liv'd, the other where they lie.

A Sonnet attributed to Shakespeare, prefixed to the second edition of Florio's translation of Montaigne's Essays 1613.

Lines 13, 14.

Shakespeare, during absence, appears to have written about the year 1600 according to Sir William Dugdale, an epitaph for the monument of Sir Thomas Stanley, Knight, which was erected in Tong Church, Salop. One half of the double epitaph is as follows :—

> " Not monumental stone preserves our fame,
> Nor sky-aspiring pyramids our name.
> The memory of him for whom this stands
> Shall outlive marble and defacers' hand :
> When all to time's consumption shall be given,
> Stanley, for whom this stands, shall stand in heaven."

Lines 13, 14.
" That when at the last great assize
All women shall together rise,
Men straight shall cast their eyes on thee.
And know at first that thou art she."—*Cowley.*

SONNET 56.

Lines 5, 6.
" My hungry eyes, though greedy, covetise
Still to behold the object of their pain."—*Spenser's Sonnets.*

SONNET 57.

Lines 6 *to* 9.

From the Dedication of the Collected Works of Shakespeare to the Lords, William, Earl of Pembroke, and Philip, Earl of Montgomery, folio, 1623 :—

" But since your L. L. have been pleased to think these trifles something heretofore, and have prosecuted both them, and their Author living, with as much favour, we hope that (they outliving him, and he not having the fate, common with some, to be executor to his own writings) you will use the like indulgence toward them, you have done unto their parent."

SONNET 58.

Lines 11, 12.
" I have given over ; I will speak no more ;
Do what you will ; your wisdom be your guide."
King Henry IV., Part 2.

SONNET 59.

Line 14.
" Make kings his subjects by exchanging verse."
I. M. S. on Shakespeare, 1632.

SONNET 60.

Line 5.
" His youth in flood."—*Troilus and Cressida.*
Lines 13, 14.
" Strong as a tower, in hope I say, Amen."—*Richard II.*

SONNET 64.

Line 1.
" Young years, conceiving, bring forth many years."
Davies to Lord Herbert.

Lines 1 to 14.

" O God ! that one might read the book of fate,
And see the revolution of the times
Make mountains level, and the continent,
Weary of solid firmness, melt itself
Into the sea ; and, other times, to see
The beachy girdle of the ocean
Too wide for Neptune's hips. How chances mock,
And changes fill the cup of alteration
With divers liquors ! Oh ! if this were seen,
The happiest youth, viewing his progress through,
What perils past, what crosses to ensue,
Would shut the book, and sit him down and die."

Second Part King Henry IV.

SONNET 65.

Lines 9, 10.

" Merely thou art death's fool ;
For him thou labourest by thy flight to shun,
And yet thou runn'st towards him still."

Measure for Measure.

SONNET 66.

Lines 1 *to* 12.

" The time is out of joint ; O cursed spite !
That ever I was born to set it right."—*Hamlet.*

" Thou whom respect of kin makes not unjust,
True noble spirit, free from hate or guile,
Thou whom thy prince hath, for thy care and trust,
Plac't for to keep the entrance of this isle :
See here th' abuses of these wicked times ;
I have exposed them open to thy view,
Thy judgment is not blinded with like crimes,
And therefore may'st perceive that all is true.
Take it ; though I seem a stranger, yet I know thee,
And for thy virtues, Pembroke, this I owe thee."

G. Withers' Dedication of " *Abuses Whipt and Stript,*" 1611.

" Virtue itself of vice must pardon beg."—*Hamlet.*

" Did I brand the times,
And myself most, in some self-boasting rhymes,
Then why this fire ?"—*Ben Jonson's Execration upon Vulcan.*

SONNET 67.

Lines 1 *to* 10.

" Now, get you to my lady's chamber, and tell her, let her paint an inch
thick, to this favour she must come."—*Hamlet.*

SONNET 68.

Lines 5 to 12.

" Thatch your poor thin roofs
" With burdens of the dead."—*Timon of Athens.*

SONNET 70.

Line 8.

" Your youth,
And the pure blood which peeps so purely throught it,
Do plainly give you out an unstained shepherd."—*Winter's Tale.*

Lines 1 to 10.

" Nor could the age have missed thee in this strife
Of vice and virtue." . . . . . .

" Whose life even those who envy it must praise,
Thou art so reverenced." . . . . . .

" But thou, whose nobless keeps one stature still,
And one true posture though besieged with ill."
Extracts from Epigram by Jonson on William Earl of Pembroke, 1616.

" It often happens that those are the best people whose characters have been most injured by slanderers ; as we usually find that to be the sweetest fruit which the birds have been pecking at."—*Swift.*

Lines 1 to 12.

" In the morn and liquid dew of youth,
Contagious blastments are most imminent :
Be wary then."—*Hamlet.*

SONNET 71.

Lines, 9, 10.

" Only compound me with forgotten dust ;
Give that which gave thee life unto the worms."
Henry IV., Part 2.

SONNET 73.

Lines 1 to 4.

" A PARADOX IN PRAISE OF A PAINTED WOMAN.
But when old age their beauty hath in chase,
And ploughs up furrows in their own smooth face ;
Then they become forsaken, and do show
Like stately abbies ruined long ago."—*Lord Pembroke's Poems.*

Line 7.
" And by and by a cloud takes all away."—*Two Gentlemen of Verona.*

Lines 9 to 12.
" He measured the flames of youth by his own dead cinders."
Greene's Never too Late, &c., 1616.

SONNET 74.

Lines 1, 2.
" Be absolute for death : either life or death
Shall thereby be the sweeter."—*Measure for Measure.*

" This fell sergeant death,
Is strict in his arrest."—*Hamlet.*

Line 11.
" Death's dishonourable victory."—*Henry IV.,* part 1.

Lines 1 to 12.
" Death makes no conquest of this conqueror,
He now lives in fame though not in life."—*Richard III.*

Line 11.
" On death, thy murderer, this revenge I take,
I slight his terror and just question make :
Which of us two the best procedure have,
Mine to this wretched world, thine to the grave."
Sir J. Beaumont, 1615.

Lines 1 to 10.
" TO A FRIEND.
" Like to a hand which hath been used to play
One lesson long, still turns the usual way :
And waits not what the hearer bids it strike,
But doth presume by custom, this will like."
Lord Pembroke's Poems.

SONNET 77.

Line 2.
"The clock upbraids me with the waste of time."—*Twelfth Night.*

Lines, 7, 8.
" The Pilot's glass
Hath told the thievish minutes how they pass."—
Alls Well that Ends Well.

SONNET 78.

Line 1.
" Muses I oft invoke your holy aid."—*Sidney's Sonnets.*

Line 3.

"Every alien pen," "a lean pen ;" this suggested the punning line in the 84th.

Line 5.

"Lo where she lies,
Whose beauty made him speak that else was dumb."—*Daniel's Sonnets.*

Lines 6, 7.

"My mistress worth gave wings unto my muse."—*Constable's Diana.*

SONNET 80.

Line 15.

"That ever I should call thee cast away."—*Antony and Cleopatra.*

SONNET 81.

Lines 5, 6.

"When I am forgotten, as I shall be,
And sleep in dull cold marble, where no mention
Of me more must be heard of."—*Henry VIII.*

Lines 7, 8.

"When I am dead, and rotten in the dust
Thou 'gin to live."—*Bishop Hall's Satires,* 1597.

Lines 8 to 14.

"Ensuing ages yet my rhymes shall cherish,
Where I emtombed my better part shall save."

Drayton's Sonnets.

Line 14.

"There is nothing liveth so in men's mouths as his name and his works," i.e., Homer's.—*Montaigne's Essays,* 1603.

SONNET 84.

Lines 7, 8.

"Would you praise Cæsar, say Cæsar, go no further."

Antony and Cleopatra.

Lines 9, 10.

"We all know that the wretched Settle was the rival of the mighty Dryden, who for a time both feared and hated him ; and Shakespeare, who appears to have been modest by nature, may have been tongue-tied by some petty poet."—*Chalmers.*

NOTES UPON SHAKESPEARE'S RIVALS,

ILLUSTRATING SONNETS 78 TO 86.

POETICAL WORKS AND DEDICATIONS REFERRED TO BY SHAKESPEARE:—

Davison's " Poetical Rhaspody," Dedicated to Lord Herbert, 1602.
Davies's " Mirum in Modum,"   do.   do.   1602.
Do. " Microcosmos," Sonnets.   do.   do.   1603.
Do. " Wits Pilgrimage,"   do.   do.   n. d.*
Do. " Humours Heaven on Earth,"   1609.
In which are evident signs of Davies being offended with Shakespeare.
Do. " Scourge of Folly,"   do.   do.   1611.
Do. " Scourge for Paper Persecutors," printed with the
          " Scourge of Folly,"   1611.

The later contains a Satire upon Shakespeare and Lord Herbert, of which notice has been given in Preliminary Observations, with Epigram 180 from the " Scourge of Folly."

REFERENCE LINES TO THE ABOVE POEMS.

SONNET 78.

" And under thee their poesy disperse."—*Davison.*

This Sonnet has reference to the following dedication, prefixed to the " Poetical Rhapsody."

" *To the most Noble, Honorable, and Worthy Lord William Earl of Pembroke, Lord Herbert of Cardiff, Marmion, and Quentin.*
" Great Earl whose high and noble mind is higher,
     And noble than thy noble high desire :
     Whose outward shape though it most lovely be,

---

* This volume is printed without date, but the poem referred to must have been written either in 1602 or 1603. T. Roe, also in the year 1603, in his " Ideas," gives an elaborate and favourable character of this Earl, for beauty, modesty, chivalry, talents, &c.

Doth in fair robes, a fairer soul attire ;
Who rich in fading wealth in endless treasures
Of virtue, valour, learning, richer art,
Whose present greatest men esteem but part
Of what by line of future hopes thy measure !
Thou worthy son unto a peerless mother !
And nephew to great Sidney of renown,
Who has deserved thy coronet, to crown
With laurel crown ; a crown excelling the other :
I consecrate these rhymes to thy great name,
Which if thou like they seek no other fame."

The devoted admirer of your Lordship's virtues, Francis Davison, (1602).

From the Sonnet-like praise in the third line it seems probable that Davison had either seen or heard of Shakespeare's addresses. The friend is everywhere proved to have been composed of all the amiable softnesses which make a woman.

SONNET 79.

" He lends thee virtue   *   *   *
     *   * Beauty doth he give."—*Davison's dedication.*

SONNET 82.

" The dedicated words which writers use."—*Davison and Davis's dedications.*

" Thou art as fair in knowledge as in hue."—*Davison and Davies's dedications.*

SONNET 83.

" The barren tender of a poet's debt."—*Davies's dedicated Sonnets :*

And the dedication of the " Mirum in Modum," 1602, in which Davies divides his broken heart between his patron and two other friends, and, as usual, evidences a painful endeavour to be highly conceited. It is to the honour of Shakespeare's patron that though this verbose rhymer aimed repeatedly at gaining the honour of his patronage, it was never granted him ; for Shakespeare, as shown, blames his friend merely for giving partial countenance to his vain, conceited, petty contemporary. Davies, failing to gain the elder brother, is far more successful in his attempt on the younger one, a man of a much lower standard of intellect. Davies, probably out of spite, dedicates a whole volume of Sonnets to him. The "Mirum in Modum" above referred to was the first dedication Davies laid before Earl William. As observed, with him he couples two of the Earl's friends; they were also his own. This is the dedicatory address :—

"To the most noble, judidious, and my best beloved Lord William, Earle of Pembroke, the most honorable Sir Robert Sidney, Knight, and the right worshipful Edward Herbert, of Montgomery, Esquire, my most honored and respected friends.

> "To subdivide souls indivisible
> (Being wholly in the whole, and in each part)
> For me were more than most impossible,
> Though I were Art itself, or more than Art.
> Yet must I make my soul a trinity,
> So to divide the same between you three ;
> For Understanding, Will, and Memory
> Makes his own soul, yet they three virtues be,
> The Understanding being first (for order so doth crave),
> And Will (good-will) the second shall receive,
> Then Memory the last shall ever have.
> And as I part my soul, my book I part
> Betwixt you three that share my broken heart."

"When others would give life and bring a tomb."—*Davies's dedicated Sonnets.*

> "Their lives more life in one of your fair eyes
> Than both your poet's can in praise devise."
> *Davies's dedicated Poem.*

SONNET 84.

"Lean penury within that pen doth dwell," *i.e., Davies.*

SONNET 86.

Davies's alluded to principally. Apply also to Sonnet 83 the following from the "Microcosmos :"—

To the Right Noble, and no less Learned than Judicious, Lord William, Earl of Pembroke, etc.

"Dear Lord, if so I could I would make known, How much I long to keep thee still alive.

These lines (though short), so long shall be thine own,
  As they have power vitality to give.
I consecrate this mite of my devotion,
  To the rich treasury of thy dear fame,
Which shall serve (though nought else worth) as a notion,
  For time to sever thy fame from thy name.
William's sons, son of William, dreaded Earl
  Of Pembroke, made by England's* dreadfull'st king,
Nephew to Sidney (rare worths, his richest pearl),
  That to this land her richest fame did bring.
These worthies worths are treasured in thee ;
  So, three in one, makes one as dear as three.

                    " To the same.

" Within my soul I sensibly do feel,
  A motion, which my mind's attraction makes :
That is, to strike love's flint against truth's steel
  More hard to kindle thy love by the sparks :
But if the fire comes not so freely forth,
  As may influence the tinder of thy love,
The tender of my zeal shall be henceforth,
  Offered in flames, that to your grace shall move ;
Which is their sphere, where they desire to rest,
  And resting there they will in glory shine,
I am thine own by double interest ;
  Sith once I vowed myself to thee and thine ;
O, then had I but single love of you,
  I should be double bound to W.
                    Your Honour's peculiar John Davies.

It was the custom of this writer in his dedicated books
to pen an epistle to the person to whom he dedicated,
which was for their eyes alone. One such volume is
extant, with an elegantly written address to the Earl of
Northumberland, in which he speaks of the difficulty he
found in 1609, of obtaining license for publication. He
was an amazing caligraphist,† which was almost his sole

---

* Henry VIII.

† It is highly probable that Herbert had received lessons in writing from
the celebrated master of the caligraphic art. This may account for the
apparent familiarity. Davies, in the same volume, in a poem, on the death
of Herbert's father, speaks of the Earl having been his friend, " My friend
did die, and so would God might I."

merit. He was writing-master to Prince Henry and numerous great personages, which may account for the freedom of his pen with the nobility. As before observed in the peculiarity of language in Sonnet 84, there appears to be allusion to this capacity of the rival. Heath, the Epigrammatist, told Davies—

> " There's none were fitter than thou to indite,
>   If thou could pen as well as thou canst write."

Such a written epistle may have been sent with the volume of Lord Herbert, which, if extant, would probably give more force to the Sonnet satires of Shakespeare.

In the "Wit's Pilgrimage,"* he addresses William Earl of Pembroke as having but of late become Earl, "That now is." After alluding to his eyes, he says:—Look, Lord, with those sharp eyes of thine (though lately open ") &c., alluding to his having just succeeded to his father's titles, and continues the poem of 50 lines to the same lord, to whom he repeatedly applies the epithet of "sweet." Harping upon the trio he struck in the last, he says—

> " Fair featured soul, well shapen upright, in which subsisting be,
>   Grace, goodness, glory; three in one, and one including three."

In the rest of the poem he gives the young Earl proverbial advice in abundance, that he may act wisely, and that the corrupt times may be bettered by his example. He concludes the poem by ardently persuading the young earl to marry. Honourable mention is made of Shake-

---

* The volume is printed uniform with the " Microcosmos," it appeared between 1603 and 1611 it being alluded to in the " Scourge of Folly." It is dedicated to Philip Herbert Earl of Pembroke, the younger brother of our poet's patron, in these words: "To the truly noble Earl, and his most honourable other half, Sir James Haies, Kn., &c." He styles the volume " Wit's Pilgrimage " (by poetical essays), through a world of Amorous Sonnets," &c., &c., the number of which is 152 ; and may been have written (being Sonnets, and as to number) in imitation of the series Shakespeare addressed to the elder brother.

speare in Davies' well-known stanzas, as well as in the
Epigram from the "Scourge of Folly," beginning, " Some
say, Good Will, &c.," inserted in the Preliminary Observations. It is but a repetition of that which he has
said in the stanzas above mentioned, and confirms what
Shakespeare said of himself, that he had become dis-
honoured by his profession, or as Davies said—

> " The stage doth stain pure gentle blood,
> Yet generous ye are in mind and mood."

Both in stanzas in the " Microcosmos " and " Humour's
Heaven on Earth," Davies alludes to Shakespeare, though
in the latter it is but to deride him.   Davies, in 1609, in
his " Humour's Heaven on Earth," denotes that our poet
had become rich : his words are, " When men have
gotten wealth they are said to be made."   (See marginal
note to stanza 79, part 2, referring especially to Shakespeare playing the King's parts in conjunction with Bur-
bage, stanza 76.   He derides them as being but " Nature's
zanies, Fortune's spite !")   The tenour is that " Fortune had
not guerdoned them their deserts " (see stanzas 76, 77, 79).
Also in the " Humour's Heaven on Earth," when de-
nouncing the enemies to a state (Part 1, stanza 244), he
adds to the word " poets " this marginal note, " A great torment in the life to come is due to those that can and will
take such an immortal revenge for any mortal injury."
This, coupled with Davies's satire, mentioned in Preliminary Observations, reveals his own opinion of his defects,
which, indeed, prove his highest honour, and of which he
himself was prophetic.   " In the Scourge for Paper Persecutors," which he feigned to be paper's complaint—that
he intended " Paper Personified " for himself (Shakespeare's
designation, Sonnet 38), is evident by the next poem in

the volume—it runs thus :—"To the right well deserved praise and honour of my dear friend, Mr. Philemon Holland, Doctor of Physic, who has given Paper no cause to complain."* From a dedication poem, every line of which tends to support all that has been advanced as to the rivalry, we gather that in 1610 or 1611, Davies was addressing his friends among the nobility, and consequently to have omitted a Sonnet address to Lord Herbert, to whom he had promised so much, would have appeared strange without apology ; hence he says :—
" Learned and judicious Lord, worthy of all Honorable Titles, for Courage, Wit, and Learning, William Earl of Pembroke."

> " Learned and judicious Lord, if I should balke,
> Thine honoured name, it being in my way ;
> My Muse unworthy were of such a walk,
> Where honor's branches make it ever May !†
> O could my might with my proportion hold,
> My May should be as glorious in effect,
> That it should work what might and glory could ;
> Wherewith thy glories still, should still be deckt.
> But though I may, I cannot wanting might,
> Which makes my May to work as cold, as bare ;
> So then (like winter) I must pinch thy right,
> Although to right thee be my Muse's care.
>   But when the sun of favour shines on me,
>   My May may then have might to flourish thee."

In the 3rd line he imitates Shakespeare in his 89th Sonnet, and, as if exampled by Shakespeare, he speaks significantly of his Muse. It is plain his vaunting vein

---

* The " Scourge of Folly " has an engraving for its title-page representing Folly scourged by the author on the back of Time. It is doubtful who the person is Davies is represented scourging. The British Museum copy is without the engraving ; so I can guess only from the contents of the volume, and should say, from a close perusal, that he may have intended it as a squib on Shakespeare.

† Referring to the supposed propitious patronage consequent on a dedication in the month of May, and his Muse's desire to keep the Earl of Pembroke's memory ever fresh and green.

is humbled.   He seems to have been quelled by Shakespeare's reproof in the 38th Sonnet, and is compelled to
admit that his Muse " wants might," the sun of favour
being withdrawn from him, his May is nipped, hence his
lines are " wintry—bare." He can offer Lord Herbert but
a meagre, wintry garland, although he conceives it is the
office of his Muse, in spite of all reproof, to give the Earl
his due ; but as another stands in his way he must await
his removal.   Then he consoles himself when he receives
the sunshine of favour, he may have power to make him
flourish.   In the last line he plainly imitates the last lines
of Shakespeare's 86th.   He also alludes to the 4th line
of the 79th, and intimates that the place then given his
Muse, she was worthy to keep, and might, as well as any
other, preserve the glory of his spring ever flourishing,
which was the peculiar office of Shakespeare's Muse.

Davies was entirely silenced by Shakespeare's reproofs,
since he, in spite of his early promises, in but the above
instance addressed the Earl till the year of Shakespeare's
death (1616), but this dedication volume, through its
excessive rarity, I have not been able to see ; but I find
from the Biblio Anglo Poetica, that the inscription opens
in his usual fantastic fashion, "To the right right noble,
for all that is in nobility, art or nature, William Earl of
Pembroke," etc.   His satire, "The Scourge of Folly," is
too long for insertion ; the reader will probably have had
quite enough with these extracts towards its conclusion.
They are given to show his jealous feeling and rivalry.

"Alas !

That e'er this dotard made me such an ass ;
To hear such, and that in such a thing
We call chronicle, so on me bring
A world of shame ; a shame upon them all,
That make mine injuries historical,

> To wear out time : that never (without end)
> My shame may last, without some one it mend.
> And if a sens'less creature (as I am
> And so am made by those whom thus I blame),
> My judgment give, from those I know it well,
> His notes for art and judgment doth excel.
> Well fare thee, man of art and world of wit,
> That by supremest mercy livest yet.
> Yet dost but live, yet liv'st thou to the end,
> But so thou past for time, which thou dost spend."

Ending with—

> "So may ye grace me with eternal lines,
>   That compass can and gage the deep'st designs."

On account of Davies taking a vulgar view of the subject, his poem, for the chief part, is but a picture of his own jealousy, rivalry, and spite, and proves, as he himself predicted, both his lasting shame and glory. In an address to the reader at the end of the volume, he apologises for his foolish " licentious reprehensions." He confesses he has taxed some with his " pen's tongue," whose " names suppressed are," he imputes his licentious writing to the change his " pleasant disposition " had received. He had been " disgraced with fell disasters," or, in other words, some shame he had received put him in a bitter mood, and instigated him to pen " The Scourge of Folly."

It is evident the satire was written in revenge for Shakespeare having made sport of him to the Earl, and under the name of Paper he pours forth his own grievances, and directs his utmost indignation against one who had obtained the patronage he himself had sought, the more so as that writer was a dramatic writer, one who was not content with his gains by the stage, but must seek to thrive better by recording the unworthy actions of a lord. Davies throughout the piece severely censures the chro-

niclers of petty events, from the historians of English
history to the relator of a living noble's "sedges," as he
derisively called them ; but what most grieved him to
the heart was to be perpetually chronicled in Shakespeare's
poetic diary, in terms only of ridicule.   He, therefore,
pens in imitation of Shakespeare a satirical poem, and
speaks sometimes in the name of Paper Personified, and
sometimes in his own name.   He mentions two disre-
putable dramatic writers, Marlowe and Greene ; the latter
he triumphantly says is "now well nigh forgot."   He
blames Shakespeare's " Venus and Adonis," for which its
author had apologised, and had redeemed himself in the
following year by penning a graver labour, " The Lucrece."
To Shakespeare Davies couples himself, admitting faults
in his own pen, which he briefly censures for its style, not
its matter ; and as a parallel to their enmity, he complains of Nash and Harvey's paper war, and blames their
" ugly satirising ;" but, in his opinion, the doctor got
the best of it.   Users of " new affected words," said to
be " the death of Poetry," are upbraided.   He instances
the word " Equipage," used by Shakespeare in Sonnet 32,
hence fortune, he avows, frowns upon poetry as a work
of darkness, whose soul is all satire.   Yet he jeeringly tells
it to be blythe to feed on air, adding—

> " But if air fat thee not as through thee it passes,
>   Live upon sentences 'gainst golden asses."

He relates how Ben Jonson and Dekker made themselves
public laughing stocks through a quarrel, and is especially
indignant at writers for the stage exalting kings to gods,
by putting majestic words into their mouths.   But of
what avail is that, he exclaims, " if for an hunger starven

fee, they foolishly make an idol of a golden ass :" he gives advice ; be scanty of praise to your kind patrons, and not for a little gain "with rich praise books to lade," such " shadowing beauty forth in other's praise " is folly, when they soon die, forgotten.   This is but an echo of Shakespeare's Sonnets 71 to 74, but this consolation is offered to those against whom his satire is levelled :—

> " You are half gods and more, so cannot die
> By reason of your wit's divinity."

They are blamed also for writing in a subtle manner, creating obscure mysteries, but their chief offence lay in penning epistles to lords.   Davies wisely points at others, lest his object should appear too obvious ; he feared to point at his great rival in too open a manner.   Davies could not see that by his own foolish verses he became the subject of his own satire.   He again and again speaks of the folly of dedicating to a lord, imputing to Shakespeare the worst of motives, for to no other can the allusion apply, no one having written as he did to a patron ; and I have reasons to suspect that Davies was prompted to this by Drayton, who, perhaps, was the intelligencer alluded to in Sonnet 86, as aiding Davies. like an evil spirit, with dark suggestions.   I partly infer this from the turn the satire takes, being a direct echo of Drayton's lines upon Shakespeare, see p. 15, and also on account of that poet being a friend of Davies's, as sonnets between them prove, but more especially as Drayton during Shakespeare's life and also after his death, appears to have been extremely jealous of him, besides the latter has several satirical allusions to him in his Sonnets before Davies appeared as a rival ; but it appears in this, as in every other instance of Shakespeare's connexion with his contemporaries, that he, like Raphael, occasioned enmity more by his merit then his manners, both being of a like gentle loving nature. Whenever Shakespeare is mentioned it is almost always either as " loving countryman," " loving good friend," "friendly Shakespeare," " gentle Shakespeare," " Sweet swan of Avon," etc.

Shakespeare cared but little whether the Sonnet writers of his day were offended, he knew the foremost wits of the time, Ben Jonson, Beaumont, and Fletcher, and others, looked upon the mistress-sonnetters with contempt, and would view his Sonnets as of a satirical tendency, and delight in the scheme. They would at once see that the Sonnets were used in an order and continuity, and with a mastery the halting sonnet-writers had never conceived, and could never equal, in regard to whom Shakespeare looked upon himself as a nightingale among a choir of common song birds.

ADDITIONAL NOTES TO SONNETS 86 TO 126.

SONNET 86.
Lines 5 to 9.
"They say thou hast a familiar spirit,
By whom thou cans't accomplish,
What thou wilt."—*Marlowe.*

Lines 5 to 10.
SATIRE TO A BAD POET.
"Great famous wit, whose rich and easy vein,
Free and unus'd to drudgery or pain,
Has all Apollo's treasury at command."—*Butler.*

Lines 13, 14.
"Then will Ajax lack matter, if he have
Lost his argument."—*Troilus and Cressida.*

SONNET 87.
Lines 13, 14.
"Or to live
But in a dream of friendship."—*Timon of Athens.*

SONNET 88.
Lines 6, 7.
"I have exchanged a real innocence,
To gain a mere fantastical report."—*Fletcher.*

SONNET 89.
Line 3.
"For you shall find she will outstrip all praise,
And make it halt behind her."—*Tempest.*

"But words came halting forth."—*Sidney's Arcadia.*

"And straight leaps forth a poet, but as lame
As Vulcan or the founder of Cripplegate."—*Jonson.*

Line 3.

CEL.   "Come, lame me with reasons."

ROS.   " Then there were two cousins* laid up ;
When the one should be lamed with reasons,
And the other mad without any."—*As you Like it.*

Line 14.
" I will never love that which my friend hates."
Much Ado about Nothing.

SONNET 90.

Lines 1 to 4.
ON ACTORS.

"They forget they are i' th' statutes, the rascals,
They are blazoned there, there they are tricked :
They and their pedigrees, they need no other herald, Sirs ;
Methinks if nothing else, yet this alone, the
Very reading of the public edicts, should
Fright thee from commerce with them, and give thee
Distaste enough of their actions."—*The Poetaster.*

SONNET 93.

Lines 1 to 2.
" Hearts that are tied together with these consecrated bonds, are like man
and wife, joined together inseparable ; no encomiums could be too lavish for
them : certainly there is nothing more ravishing upon earth than a friendship
thus entertained. It is indeed that which surmounts the possibility of an
exact description, and reserves its full discovery to the prize of experience."
The Gentleman's Calling, 1682,
By the Author of the " Whole Duty of Man."

Lines 1 to 12.
" The vow of marriage may be properly considered as a vow of perpetual
indissoluble friendship. It is easy by pursuing the parallel between friendship and marriage to show how exact a conformity there is between them ;
to prove that all the precepts laid down with respect to the contraction, and
the maxims advanced with regard to the effects of friendship are true of
marriage, in a more literal sense and a stricter interpretation."
Sermon by J. Taylor, LL.D., 1700.

Lines 1 to 14.
SONNET OF FRIENDSHIP.
" Friendship on earth, we may as easily find
As he, the North East Passage, that is blind !
Sophistical affection is the best
This age affords, no friend abides the test :

---

* Two cousins, meaning also two cozens, *i.e.*, cheats.

They make a glorious show a little space,
But tarnish in the rain like copper lace.
So by degrees when we embrace so many,
We courted are like whores, not lov'd of any.
Choose one of two companions of thy life,
Then be as true as thou woulds't have thy wife ;
Though he live joyless that enjoys no friend,
He that hath many pays for't in the end."

William Earl of Pembroke.

Lines 12, 13.
" Bear a fair presence, although your heart be tainted."

Comedy of Errors.

Lines 1 to 14.
" Two pictures of a married life,
I look on thee, and thought of thee,
In vastness and in mystery ;
And of thy spirit as of a wife."—*In Memoriam.*

SONNET 95.
Line 14.
" Lilies that fester smell far worse than weeds."—*Edward III.*, 1597.

SONNET 96.
Lines 13, 14.

Shakespeare elsewhere repeats himself, using word for
word. Thus in the "Taming of the Shrew," the line
"Pisa renowned for grave citizens," is repeated in the 1st
and 4th acts.

SONNET 97.
Lines 1 to 4.
" If, as I say, I compare it all unto the four years, I so happily enjoyed the
sweet company and dear, dear society of that worthy man, it is nought but a
vapour ; nought but a dark and irksome night, since the time I have lost
him, which I shall ever hold a bitter day."—*Montaigne's Essays, Edit.* 1603.

SONNET 98.
Lines 1 to 6.
" Then came fair May, the fairest maid on ground.
Lord ! how all creatures laught when her they spied,
And leap'd and danced as they had ravished been."

Fairy Queen.

Lines 5 to 14.

"What art thou then? I cannot guess:
But though I seem in star and flower
To feel thee—some diffusive power,
I do not therefore love thee less."—*In Memoriam.*

SONNET 99.

Lines 1 to 5.

"The rose and expectancy of the fair state,
A violet in the youth of primy nature;
Forward, not permanent; sweet, not lasting."—*Hamlet.*

Line 7.

"Marjoram comforteth the brain."—*Hyl.*

"The soft marjoram."—*Peacham* (1613).

Lines 1 to 14.

"My ladie's presence makes the roses red,
Because to see her lips they blush for shame;
The lilies' leaves, for envy, pale become,
And her white hands in them this envy bred;
The marigold abroad the leaves doth spread,
Because the sun's and her power is the same;
The violet of purple colour came,
Dy'd with the blood she made my heart to shed:
In brief—all flowers from her their virtue take:
From her sweet breath their sweet smells do proceed."
              Constable's Diana.

SONNET 100.

Lines 1 to 4.

In a conversation between Shakespeare and Ben Jonson, recorded in Lansdowne's "Essays on Poetry" (1721), Ben is said to have asked Shakespeare why he wrote historical plays. He replied, that finding the people generally very ignorant of history, he wrote them in order to instruct them in that particular, which this Sonnet seems to confirm.

"I thought all words were lost that were not spent on thee."
              Sidney's Sonnets.

Line 7.

"Our Shakespeare wrote, too, in an age as blest,
The happiest poet of his time, and best;
A gracious prince's favour cheer'd his Muse,
A constant favour he ne'er fear'd to lose."—*Otway.*

Lines 1 to 8.

" Elizabeth to his lays open'd her royal ear,
  Yet he does not drop from his honied verse
  One sable tear."—*Chettle of Shakespeare*, 1603.

SONNET 102.

Lines 7 to 12.

" The crow doth sing as sweetly as the lark
  When neither is attended ; and I think
  The nightingale, if she should sing by day,
  When every goose is cackling, would be thought
  No better a musician than the wren."—*Merchant of Venice.*

SONNET 103.

Lines 9, 10.

" Striving to better, oft we mar what's well."—*King Lear.*

SONNET 104.

Lines 9 to 12.

" The fixure of her eye hath motion in it."—*Winter's Tale.*

SONNET 105.

Lines 1, 2.

" Thy image should be sung, for thou that goddess art
  Which only we without idolatry adore."—*Constable's Diana.*

Lines 1 to 4.

"To my Muse.

" Away and leave me, thou thing most abhorred,
  That hast betrayed me to a worthless lord,
  Made me commit most fierce idolatry
  To a great image through thy luxury.'
    *Extract from an Epigram by Jonson, evidently levelled at
      Shakespeare, his patron lord, and Muse.*

Line 4.

" Only in you my song begins and endeth."—*Sidney's Sonnets.*

" One will I serve."—*Motto of the Pembroke Family.*

" Man praises man ; and Garrick's memory next,
  When time hath somewhat mellowed it, and made
  The idol of our worship while he lived
  The god of our idolatry once more,
  Shall have an altar."—*Cowper.*

SONNET 106.

Line 4.

" Fit for such ladies and such lovely knights."—*Fairy Queen.*

Lines 9, 10.

" Miracle of the world, I never will deny
That former poets praise the beauty of their days ;
But all those beauties were but figures of thy praise,
And all those poets did of thee but prophecy."

Constable's Diana.

SONNET 107.

Lines 5 to 8.

" Alack ! our terrene moon
Is now eclipsed, and it portends alone
The fall of Antony."—*Antony and Cleopatra.*

Lines 5 to 14.

" Pembroke to court (to which thou wert made strange) ;
Go, do thy homage to thy sovereign ;
Weep and rejoice for this sad joyful change,
Then weep for joy, thou need'st not tears to feign,
Such late thine eyes did naught else entertain,
If I mistake thee not ; and thy best part,
Thy virtues, will thy liege's favour gain,
For virtue virtue loves, as art doth art,
Then will he love thee, loved for thy desert."

Davies' Microcosmos, 1603.

SONNET 108.

Lines 1 to 4.

" What can I write that hath not yet been said ?
What have I said that others have not affirmed ?
What is approved that ought to be assayed ?
Or what is vowed that shall not be performed ?"

Paradise of Dainty Devices.

" What should I say ?—what yet remains to do ?"—*Drayton's Sonnets.*

Lines 8, 9.

" With ditties so sensibly expressing Amphialus' case that every word
seemed to be but a diversifying of the name of Amphialus."—*Sidney's
Arcadia.*

SONNET 109.

Lines 1 to 5.

" Friendships are marriages of the soul, and of fortunes and interests and
counsels.—*Jeremy Taylor's Measures of Friendship.*

Lines 1 to 6.

"For when men have contracted friendship, and espoused their souls and minds to one another, there arises a new relation between them, for in this close and new relation men give each other a property in themselves."

Whole Duty of Man.

SONNET 110.

Lines 1 to 4.

Shakespeare, in 1603, condescended to grace with his presence the "Sejanus" of Jonson, upon its first appearance upon the stage. This was at the Globe, to which Shakespeare belonged, by this our poet seemed desirous to give his rival a fair chance of applause; but on this occasion, in spite of even Shakespeare's presence, more murmurs than plaudits were raised. It is remarkable that Drayton, in his 47th Sonnet, makes direct allusion to the Globe Playhouse, "the proud round," where he sat, as he himself says, an envious observer of other's fame; but Shakespeare, who could have made triumphal allusion to it, is silent.

SONNET 111.

Lines 1 to 4.

"Players, I love ye, and your quality,
　As ye are men that pass time not abused;
And [W.S. R.B.] some I love for painting poesy,
　And say fell fortune cannot be excused
That hath for better uses you refused
　Wit, courage, good shape, and all good,
So long as all these goods are no worse used:
　And though the stage doth stain pure gentle blood,
Yet generous ye are in mind and mood."

On Shakespeare and Richard Burtage—J. Davies' Microcosmus, 1603.

SONNET 112.

Lines 1 to 12.

"The censure of which one must in your allowance outweigh an whole theatre of others."—*Hamlet.*

Lines 1 to 12.

" In so thick and dark an ignorance as now almost covers the age, I crave leave to stand near your light, and by that light to be read."—*Jonson's Dedication of Catiline to Lord Pembroke*, 1616.

" None can move
Shakespeare out of Adonis' grove,
There sullenly he sits."—*Davenport*, 1650.

Lines 5 to 14.

" I, from the blind and faithless world aloof,
Nor fear its envy nor desire its praise,
But choose my path through solitary ways."
M. Angelo, Sonnet.

SONNET 113.

Line 14.

" It is mine (my eyne ?) or Valentine's praise."
Two Gentlemen of Verona.

Lines 1 to 14.

" My love talked with rocks and trees ;
He finds on misty mountain ground
. His own sweet shadow glory crown'd,
He sees himself in all he sees."—*In Memoriam.*

SONNET 114.

Lines 1 to 4.

" Mine eye too great a flattery for my mind."—*Twelfth Night.*

Line 6.

" A sompnour was with us in that place,
That hadde a fire-red cherubinne face ?"
Chaucer, Canterbury Tales.

" Nos grands docteurs au cherubin visage."
Old French Ep.

SONNET 116.

Lines 1 to 14.

" The love of men to women is a thing common and of course, but the friendship of man to man infinite and immortal."—*Allot's Wit's Commonwealth*, 1598.

SONNET 117.

Lines 1 to 4.

" There belongs to this religion of friendship certain due rites and decent ceremonies, as visits, messages, missives, &c.—*Howel's Familiar Letters.*

Line 5.

" Garrick, who long was married to the town,
At length a fashionable husband grown,
Forsakes his spouse : base man ! for, truth to tell,
She loved her own dear Davy wondrous well."

Prologue to the Contract. Foote, 1776.

Lines 1 to 14.

" All thy vexations

Were but my trials of thy love, and thou
Hast strangely stood the test."—*Tempest.*

SONNET 118.

Lines 1 to 14.

."Cordials of pity give me now,
  For I too weak for purgings strow."—*Cowley's Mistress.*

Lines 1 to 8.

" Surfeit is the father of much fast."—*Measure for Measure.*

SONNET 119.

Lines 1, 2.

" This Troilus in teares 'gan distill
As licour out of Allambike full fast."

Chaucer's Troilus and Cressida, v. 432.

Line 7.

" The poet's eye, in a fine frenzy rolling,
Doth glance from earth to heaven."

Midsummer Night's Dream.

Line 10.

" Sweet are the uses of adversity."—*As You Like it.*

SONNET 120.

Lines 1 to 14.

" So in the rites of friendship as of love,
Suspicion is not seldom an improper
Advantage, for the knitting faster joints
Of faithfullest affection."—*Massinger.*

Lines 13, 14.

" As you from crimes would pardoned be,
Let your indulgence set me free."—*Tempest.*

SONNET 121.

Lines 1 to 6.

" Friendship is a divine excellency wrapt up in a common name, and nothing less than the uttermost perfection of flesh and blood for wisdom and virtue can entitle a man to the character of a true friend."—*Sir R. L'Estrange.*

Line 9.

" I care not so much what I am with others as I respect what I am with myself."—*Montaigne's Essays,* 1603.

Lines 1 to 4.

" Virtue itself scapes not calumnious strokes."—*Hamlet.*

SONNET 123.

Lines 1 to 4.
" My happy verse,
The strong built trophies of her living fame."
Drayton's Sonnets.

Lines 2, 3.
" Ev'ry song shall be
A pyramid b...lt to thy memory."
W. Brown to Lord Pembroke, 1613.

SONNET 124.

Lines 13, 14.
" They hate for ever, who have lov'd for hours."
W. A. Earl of Stirling.

SONNET 125.

Lines 1, 2.
" When my outward actions doth demonstrate
The native act and figure of my heart,
In complement extern."—*Othello.*

SONNET 126.

Lines 5, 6.
" This good being done,
The hand could pluck her back that shov'd her on."
Antony and Cleopatra.

Lines 11, 12.
" Nature that made thee with herself at strife,
Saith that the world hath ending with thy life."
Venus and Adonis.

" Shakespeare with whom
Quick nature died."—*Monumental Epitaph.*

SONNET 127.

FROM the original edition of Lord Herbert's poems printed in 1660, we learn that this nobleman, later in life, also formed a poetical friendship with Sir Benjamin Ruddyard, Knt.,* in conjunction with whom the greater number of the poems were written, being answered by the latter by way of repartee. There are also several distinct poems, written by them apart. The poems by Herbert are signed P, as a safeguard to authenticity. That this lord was worthy the name of a poet, and that the best poem imputed to him was really by him, we have the authority of William Brown, author of " Britannia's Pastorals."

Jonson, also in 1621, attests his ability to use his pen, in these lines from a masque presented at court—

> " You know how to use your sword and your pen,
> And you love not alone the arts, but the men ;
> The graces and Muses ev'ry where follow
> You, as you were their second Apollo."†

* Jonson addresses this knight in three of his Epigrams, and in these he extols his " holiest friendship," and also his " learned muse," and questions which is his chief merit—
> " Writing thyself, or judging others writ."

† Jonson also denotes that the King loved him for the chaste example he set the court.

Pembroke and Ruddyard have pleasant attacks upon "painted women." Among them is one in which P is the man and R is the woman. P also writes "an ironical praise of his mistress." One of the poems written by this lord is entitled "A Paradox : that beauty lies not in women's faces, but in lover's eyes," and bears a strong resemblance to a remarkable passage in "Troilus and Cressida," a late play, and one which Shakespeare appears to have written for his patron friend, as the preface to the edition of 1609 intimates that it was written for some noble personage for private use. Some of the headings of Pembroke's Sonnets are as follows :—

"That lust is not his aim."
"On one heart made of two."
"That he would not be beloved."
"I left you and now the gain of yon is a double gain."

Pembroke and Ruddyard have also long serious dialogues upon "Love and Reason." Pembroke is "Sir Love," Ruddyard, "Reason." They thus conduct their argument:

"R. 'And now to you, Sir Love, your love I crave,
    Of you no mastery I desire to have ;
    But that we may like honest friends agree,
    Let us to reason, fellow servants be.'
P. 'Love here the husband is, reason the wife,
    Not grudging at her husband's active sway,
    But thinks she rules so just laws to obey.
    He is no mountebank, his wares do teach,
    Beyond the setting forth of any speech :
    Nor alchemist, but that elixir old,
    Which turns lust mercury, to friendship gold.'
R. 'Whenever you can love to reason marry,
    I will not from that happy wedding tarry."

Their long argument ends thus :—

"Yet for all this we will not disagree,
    Each lover thinks none ever lov'd but he ! "

Pembroke has a poem "To his mistress, of his friend's opinion of her, and his answer to his friend's objection, with his constancy towards her." This is the first stanza:

> "One with admiration told me,
> He did wonder much and marvel,
> (As by chance he did behold thee)
> How I could become so servile,
> To thy beauty, which he swears,
> Every ale house lattice wears."

Among various ironical Sonnets "To his Mistress" on painting, he has one to her in which he declares that the sole occasion of his love for her is on account of her false adornments.

Ruddyard and Pembroke were schoolfellows together at Oxford; he married a relative of the Earl of Pembroke. This would account for the nearness of their friendship. In the poems which they wrote in conjunction, the task is invariably assigned to Ruddyard of replying to his lordship's romantic ideas—they both alike favoured poets and learned men. There is no clue to the date of their writing together, but it was prior to 1615.

We must not omit to observe that Clarendon in his "History of the Rebellion" has drawn a noble portrait of Lord Pembroke, pourtraying him as a most liberal and accomplished courtier; yet while paying him the highest compliments, he admits his defects. He says he was a lover of women, but it was their wit rather than their beauty by which he was charmed; but for his defects Clarendon offers sufficient plea. The difference between the comments of Shakespeare and Clarendon upon this lord is, that one reveals allegorically the sunrise of his early virtuous manhood, the other, the sunset of his

P

years, somewhat obscured by the cloud of blighted hope,
yet of a dazzling radiance. Clarendon also bears testimony
to his great zeal for friendship, which he marks as a
distinguishing feature of his character.

It is worthy of observation that though Sidney wrote
passages in the "Arcadia" upon the folly of poets sonnetting their angry loves, yet he himself fell into the same
folly ; but it was not so with Shakespeare, for he remained constant to his doctrine.

SONNET 134.
Lines 1 to 14.
"To Fantasie.

"I gave my faith to love, love his to me,
That he and I sworn brothers should remain ;
Thus faith received faith given back again :
Who could imagine bond more sure could be,
Love flies to her, yet holds he my faith taken ;
And from my virtue raising my offence,
Making me guilty of my innocence ;
And only bond for being so forsaken.
He makes her ask what I before had vowed,
Giving her that which he had given to me,
I bound by him, and he by her made free,
Whoever so hard breach of faith allowed.
Speak you which should of right and wrong discuss,
Was right ere wronged, or wrong ere righted thus."—*Drayton.*

SONNET 140.
Lines 9 to 12.

This is evidently a parody upon such Sonnets as
Drayton's 9th, headed "Loves Lunacy," in which he
avouches his own madness.

SONNET 141.
Lines 1 to 13.
" 'Tis very true, I thought you as fair,
As women in th' idea are."

" Nay, but when the world but knows how false you are,
There's not a man will think you fair." —*Cowley's Mistress* "*Not Fair.*"

SONNET 142.

Lines 1, 2.

" If that be sin, which in love's heart doth breed,
A loathing of all loose unchastitie,
Then love is sin, and let me sinful be."—*Sidney to Stella.*

SONNET 143.

Lines 1 to 9.

" Love, like a shadow flies when substance love pursues,
Pursuing that which flies, and flying what pursues."

Merry Wives of Windsor.

Lines 1 to 12.

" So holy and so perfect, is my love,
And I in such a poverty of grace,
That I shall think it a most plenteous crop,
To glean the broken ears after the man,
That the man's harvest reaps ; loose now and then
A scattered smile, and that I'll live upon."

As You Like it.

SONNET 144.

Lines 1 to 8.

" An evil spirit, your beauty, haunts me still,
Wherewith, alas ! I have been long possest,
Which ceases not to tempt me to each ill,
Nor gives me once but one poor minute's rest.
Thus am I still provoked to every evil
By this good wicked spirit, sweet angel-devil."

Drayton's 24th Idea.

Line 3.

" Brutus, as you know, was Cæsar's angel."—*Julius Cæsar.*

SONNET 145.

Lines 13, 14.

" Your love and hate is this, I now do prove you ;
Your love is hate, by hate to make me love you."

Drayton's Sonnets.

SONNET 146.

Lines 4 to 7.

" I have heard of your paintings too, well enough : God hath given
you one face, and you make yourselves another."—*Hamlet.*

Line 12.
" I will begin the fashion
Less without and more within."—*Cymbeline.*

Line 14.
" Kill'd like to slaves, and cannot kill again."—*Fletcher's Bonduca.*

Line 14.
" Struck dead at first, what needs a second striking ?"
Venus and Adonis.

SONNET 147.
Lines 1 *to* 8.
" Your affections are
A sick man's appetite, who desires that most
Which would increase his evil."—*Coriolanus.*

Lines 9 *to* 12.

In this the poet appears to level at such sonnetteering as Drayton's 38th, in which there is an argument between love and reason for supremacy. This poet also addresses his mistress (Sonnet 9), and seriously tells her he has been nine years deranged. He begins thus :—

" I will resolve you I am lunatic,
Thus talking idly in this bedlam fit,
And bedlam like, thus raving in my grief."

SONNET 148.
Line 12.
" The sun not yet thy sighs from heaven clears."—*Romeo and Juliet.*

SONNET 151.
Line 9.
" My heart shall be
The faithful compass that still points to thee."—*Gray.*

SONNET 153.
" Thine eye darts forth the fire that burneth me."—*Venus and Adonis.*

Line 14.
" At whose pure eyes Love lights his hallowed fire."
Drayton's Sonnets.

SONNET 154.
Lines 3, 4.
" And all the greekish girls shall tripping sing."
Troilus and Cressida.

Line 8.
"Thus was I, sleeping, by a brother's hand
Of life, of crown, of queen, at once dispatched."—*Hamlet.*

REMARKS UPON NOTES.

Many more extracts might have been brought forward
from the dramas and poems of Shakespeare illustrative of
the duo-uno idea so frequently recurring in the Sonnets,
and, in fact, their very theme throughout. Shakespeare
has more such passages embracing this idea than all the
writers of his own age put together, and perhaps more
than all other secular writers.

In 1601, during the period of his writing the Sonnets,
he wrote a most remarkable poem, involving this theme
in its entirety, called "The Phœnix and Turtle," for
Robert Chester's "Love's Martyr, or Rosalin's Complaint,"
allegorically shadowing the truth of love in the constant
fate of the Phœnix and Turtle. Shakespeare's mystical
lines, beginning with—

" Let the bird of loudest lay "

are now to be found appended to the "Passionate Pilgrim." The idea or theme arises from a poetical legal
view of marriage law, the husband and wife, though
twain, being considered but one.

THE LOVE OF SIR PHILIP SIDNEY

FOR PENELOPE DEVEREUX,

AND

LADY RICH'S ILLICIT AMOURS REVEALED.

PRESUMING that the readers may desire to know something more of Sidney's love for the lady whom he has
immortalised, and that lady's love for Sidney, and afterwards for others, and to show that which very likely caused
Shakespeare to dislike sonnetting, and also probably gave
rise to the allegory, and to give its application to the last
twenty-eight Sonnets,* as a satire upon corrupt wedded
love, I have penned these remarks.

Penelope Devereux, the lady whose love Sidney so
heedlessly lost and then so rashly strove to win, was at
once both his bliss and bane ; the ornament of her times and
their blackest disgrace. She it was, whose darkest shades
(for which, however, apology can be made) were used to
set off the bright picture Shakespeare paints of his friend.
Her history belongs to the secret history of the times. Sir
Philip Sidney and Penelope Devereux were truly a pair of
" star-crost lovers." The end of her brother's life (the earl
of Essex), though in another way, was equally disgraceful
with hers. All Sidney's misfortunes may be attributed to

---

* As remarked, these Sonnets were not intended to represent her loving
alone, but as a satire on the times, though she is chiefly alluded to.

his passion for Penelope; losing her he lost all, and seemed utterly regardless of his honour and life.

Her history, which makes truth seem far stranger than fiction, remains to be fully told. The outline of it will show the truth of Shakespeare's pictures of her late in life, and contrast with Sidney's descriptions of her in her budding beauties and seeming virtues. The extreme folly of Sidney, blasting his reputation in Sonnets, Shakespeare justly ridicules; but Sidney's fame becoming brighter and brighter, and setting in glory, received national homage; while the fame of the mistress of his song became darker and darker, and ended in the deepest shame. The impartial reader will, however, see that her fate deserves pity, and that Sidney's heedless loving, which he himself blames, merits censure. There were faults on either side, neither knowing, till too late, their own mind.

It was early decided by the friends of Sidney and those of Penelope that Sidney should marry her. She was extremely beautiful and witty, and was viewed as a fit mate for him. But her beauty had made her wayward and proud, and Sidney was not in such haste to marry as her friends desired him to be. This was in 1576, when he was twenty-two years of age, and she was fifteen. He was at this time devoted to his studies, and becoming a friend of Spenser's, he for a time forgot Penelope, and she, perhaps, indignant at his neglect, and at the suggestion of ill-advised friends, accepted the love of Lord Robert Rich, a man altogether unworthy of her. He is described as being of a most mean despicable nature. Had he been capable of so much felicity, he would have become possessor of the love of this heaven of joy. But what was such purity and beauty to one of such a debased nature as her husband proved. By her marriage with Lord Rich, rich not only in name, but in immense wealth, she was at once the cause of mutual grief and sin. Sidney lost his peace of mind for life, and sought despairingly and futilely to gain her love (though but delusively in verse), which he saw was in reality lost to him for ever, as she was another's, and what another's—"Hyperion to a Satyr." Sidney lost the foremost beauty, Penelope—the foremost wit of which those chivalrous times could boast. Robert Lord Rich could not estimate the value of that Rose of Beauty, that pearl of price of which he became the reckless possessor. He did not see, as her poet-lover did, that the sum of all wealth was the possession of her. He did not seek to gain her love, nor did she give him hers, and though she was true to him, she loved him not.

Sidney to beguile his grief retired to Wilton, and commenced writing that quaint though charming romance, the "Arcadia." His sister Mary, Countess of Pembroke, desired him to pen this work to divert him from his sorrows, and to this lady he dedicated the volume. Sidney has pourtrayed Penelope in it as the principal heroine, arrayed in all her supremacy of beauty, as Philoclea; he also shadowed himself under the appellation of Philisides, in the discourses of these lovers he devised to embody his own passion. But his overcharged heart was forced to give vent to his feelings in another channel. He desired another subject to invent ; what should he pen to give respite to his woe ?—His Muse exclaimed—

"Fool, look in thy heart and write."

And that which he wrote was printed in 1591, five

years after his death, under the title of "Astrophel and Stella." Sidney is Astrophel, and Lady Rich is Stella. Sidney resolved, nay, felt compelled, in spite of his conscience, to "Joy therein" and proclaim his love, "though nations count it shame," (*Sonnet* 28;) and he asks himself in the 34th, "whether he is not ashamed to publish his disease?" "No," he says, "it being so rare, it will bring him fame; and lest wise men should view his loving as folly, he will write close, that is, in a riddle-like way, so that none seeing his drift, he will offend none;" he thus resolved to address Sonnets, 108 in number, to another man's wife, and in them to deride her husband as a "Rich fool," an expression which he again and again repeats, and his only excuse is, that her husband is not worthy of her, nor does he trat her worthily. In one Sonnet he exclaims—

> "But that Rich fool, who by blind fortune's lot,
> The richest gem of love and life enjoys,
> And can with foul abuse such beauties blot ;
> Let him deprived of sweet and unfelt joys,
> (Exiled for aye from those high treasures, which
> He knows not) grow in only folly rich."—*Sonnet* 22.

And again, he says, though she is rich in beauty, nature, wit, and

> "Rich in those gifts which give th' eternal crown ;
> Who though most rich in these and ev'ry part,
> Which makes the patents of true earthly bliss,
> Hath no misfortune, but that Rich she is."—*Sonnet* 37.

Such was Sidney's excuse for his passion, and to some extent he might claim her love as his own by right, though another's, for he had long been taught to view her as reserved for him alone.

Two years after Penelope's marriage, Sidney married the daughter of Sir Francis Walsingham, yet, according

to Sidney's confession and the assertions of others, his
heart remained with Stella.   Sidney tells us that Stella's
love for him, and his love for her grew stronger, after they
were divided by marriage, than it had been before.
Sidney's wife devoted her love to her husband to the
last; she was never poisoned with jealousy, she possessed
one whom she sincerely loved, and, perhaps, even sym-
pathised with for his grievous loss.   To be the wife of
Sidney was her heart's sole desire; * and after his death,
she permitted Spenser, in a panegyric upon Sidney,
to address her as Stella, that the world might not cast
any aspersion upon Sidney's fair name, as he had become glorified by a heroic and patriotic death.

Had Sidney taken his friend Languet's constant advice
to find a wife, he would not have penned these Sonnets,
which have brought shame upon him; nor need he have
blamed himself in his 18th Sonnet, for having allowed
his best days to slip before he married; neither need he
have called on " Lordings " to listen—

> " For of my life I must a riddle tell."

The simple solution to which is, that he loved a lady who
richly excelled all others in rich gifts, but whose great
misfortune was that she was Rich   Sidney himself tells
us in Sonnet 2, that he knew not at first whether he loved
her or not—

> " I saw and liked, I liked and loved not,"

and that by his delay he lost his chance, so that Penelope
was not so much to blame, and it was her pure, though

---

* To the 1633 edition of the Arcadia, there are added certain Sonnets
written by Sir Philip Sidney, never before printed.   Among them are four
" made when his lady had a pain in her face."   They are not addressed to
Stella, but appear to be written to his wife, in as painful a mood as the
subject demanded.

blighted love for him, that won his soul to sing her praise. He then resolved, as he says—

> "To make myself believe that all is well,
> While, with a feeling skill, I paint my hell!"

For this reason he determined to write alone of her (Sonnet 3), and to virtuously love her (Sonnet 4) ; truth and beauty being virtue, it was virtuous for him to love her (Sonnet 5) ; and when he said he loved her, it was a real grief (Sonnet 6), and she appeared in mourning, by reason of her dark eyes, for her lover's fruitless love (Sonnet 7) ; and he then told her how it was that he must still love her (Sonnet 8). The idea evolved in this Sonnet, Shakespeare has varied in his 153rd and 154th Sonnets. In Sonnet 9 it is Stella's eyes that have inflamed Sidney's heart ; and in this way he goes on, idea after idea. In Sonnet 11 he says he has played the baby in her eyes, but has not sought to get into her heart. In the 13th Sonnet he says that even he could not have won her heart easily. In the 14th he blames his love, but declares it to be chaste. In the 15th Sonnet, in self-excuse, he says, any poet beholding Stella would praise her. In the 17th Sonnet, her brows are the bows with which Cupid shot him to the heart. Thus he goes on excusing and urging his love, but in Sonnet 19 his words are spent in vain ; since he can never win her, though he has her love, as she is the wife of another. He says—

> "My best wits still their own disgrace invent."

And though he felt that it was a crime to write love-verses to her, yet his grief and passion were too much for him.*

---

* He tells us he used his utmost effort to conquer his passion, but failed in the attempt, his desire triumphed over his conscience.

Penelope, on her part, though the wife of a husband she had just cause to hate, yet resolved to remain true to him, and sought by example and entreaty to teach Sidney virtue and prudence. In the 69th Sonnet Sidney joyfully says that he possesses her heart, and so may say that she is his; but he says she gave it only on condition—

"While virtuous course I take."

And he declares that though they sometimes had private interviews, yet their loves were pure. In the 83rd Sonnet we are told in a riddle-like way though the solution is simple, that she possessed a bird, that she lovingly called Sir Phip; it loved to nestle in her soft white bosom, and to be billing her lips. Her lover implies by this that her bird has favours which he is denied ; but Stella is so modest, that Sidney tells the bird to desist, lest in her virtue she should wring its neck. In one Sonnet he speaks of a kiss he stole from her while she slept, and that kiss transported him into ecstacies. In other Sonnets he affects to have changed situation with the bird, to be it, and thus delusively receives loving favours. He pleads, in a puzzling way, for the bird, implying that though it playfully bites her, it is but in loving sport.

While Sidney lived, she deserved the praises he gave her for her virtue and beauty, and his sister, the Countess of Pembroke, spoke of his " love lays" to Stella as merely " merry riddles." She would not see a fault in her beloved brother ; and his having written them to a married woman before, and very probably many of them after his own marriage was a fault innocently overlooked by her. She might have said, in her chaste religious spirit, " To the pure all things are pure."

Lady Rich, while Sidney lived, gave scandal no tongue, but after his death, either through excessive grief, or hate of her lord, she forsook the path of virtue and fair fame, and eventually her husband behaved cruelly to her ; abandoned her, though not without just cause, and treated her in a manner that drove her to despair and revenge. Neglected by her husband for years, she, following his example, transferred her affections to another : she gave her love to Mountjoy, afterwards Earl of Devonshire, who doated upon her, and after some years married her. But disaster now followed disaster. Elizabeth banished her the Court ; but upon James coming to the crown she and Lord Mountjoy came again into high favour. Scandal however, followed her, and the illegality of her marriage with the earl while her husband was still living, which had just been effected to put a good colour upon their illicit loving, was discussed ; and the king, exceedingly wrathful, told Mountjoy that he had "purchased a fair woman with a black soul," and though Mountjoy, in a letter to the King, showed legal reasons* sufficient to show his right to marry her, it would not avail. This was more than he could bear : he retired from Court, and was soon after taken with a severe illness, consequent on his excessive grief, and died. His wife attended him to the last, and never survived this disgrace ; she died shortly after, in 1606. A relative of Mountjoy declared she had brought shame upon her and her whole kindred. It would seem that Mountjoy, though deluded with the belief,

---

* Heylin says that Mountjoy, having had some children by the lady before she actually separated from the bed of Rich, conceived he might make them legitimate by this subsequent marriage.

was not her only lover. It also appears, during the latter years of the time she spent under the roof of her first husband, that he was not so much the tyrant as tyrannized over; for she, at her own option, sometimes left her husband's roof, and returned again to it; and upon her first fit of love for Mountjoy, she left her husband to live with him, and upon his being sent, by order of the Queen, to Ireland to aid Essex to suppress the rebellion, she returned to her husband, though but to leave him on Mountjoy's return; and as remarked, she was not indifferent to the proffered love of others, though in a more guarded way. So, taking her for all in all, possibly no woman ever presented two such contrasted pictures, both in feature and in morals: she was radiant fair, yet intensely dark in the lustrous depth of her black eyes; she was, while Sidney lived, an example of virtue; after his death, blot upon blot darkened her illicit loving, till she sunk, like a luminous star, from dazzling radiance to oblivious infamy.

Among the dedication Sonnets appended to the " Microcosmos," I find one that has long nestled in its hiding-place, written by that prolific penman, John Davies of Hereford, and as it relates to Stella, and is interesting, it is put before the reader. In the opening lines he alludes to the manner in which Sidney had descanted upon her name :—

> "To THE RIGHT NOBLE LADY, LADY RICH.
>
> " To descant on thy name as others do
>   (Since it is fit t' express thine excellence),
> I should, dear lady, but attend unto
>   That which to it compared is indigence.
> Yet to be rich was to be fortunate,
>   As all esteem'd ; and yet, though so thou art,

Thou wast much more than most unfortunate,
  Though richly well thou playd'st that hapless part ;
Thou didst express what art could never show,
  The soul's true grief for loss of her love's soul,
Thine action speaking passion made ; but oh !
  It made thee subject to a jail's controul :
But such a jail-bird, heavenly nightingale,
For such a cause sings best in greatest bale."

Davies in the opening lines makes allusion to her
unfortunate marriage, and in the closing lines to her
soul's deep grief for the loss of her beloved, though
also unfortunate, brother Essex, who in 1601 paid the
penalty of his rash rebellious act ; and she, in her urgent
endeavour to obtain his pardon and liberty, was herself
detained in prison for a brief period, where she, Davies
tells us, made, like the nightingale with its breast against
a thorn, a doleful sweet lamentation. Both brother and
sister were equally unfortunate, though each had received
the highest honours; one as the favourite mistress of a great
poet, the other as the favourite courtier of a great queen.

In the poem by Anne Bradstreet, already mentioned
she looks upon Sidney's sonnetting Lady Rich as a blot
on his fair fame, though she offers no excuse for her idol ;
but as beautiful poems, she gives them high praise. She
undoubtedly reports the current opinion as to Sidney and
Stella. She speaks of England's halcyon days, when Sidney
wore the laurel crown, an honour to our British soil—

  " Witness Arcadia, penn'd in his youth."

Having spoken fully of all to his praise, she refers to
" his love for Stella" as his dispraise. She says she
" honours him for what is honourable, but leaves the
rest as most unprofitable." His wiser days condemned
his " witty works." It is interesting to know that Sidney
repented of his folly. She says of his love for Lady Rich :—

> " Which makes severe eyes but scorn thy story,
>   And modest maids and wives blush at thy glory ;
>   Yet he's a little head that can't descry
>   A world of treasure in that rubbish, lye."

She has only grave doubts about Stella :—

> " Illustrious Stella, thou didst shine full well
>   If thine aspect was mild to Astrophel."

She will but slightly blame her idol Sidney ; since, as
the reader has seen (ante p. 163), the utmost blame is
given to his poor mistress.   She was to him a comet of
ill omen, and afterwards proved the shame of her sex.
The poetess declares she had thought better of Sidney,
but as others have fallen, gods and men, he must be forgiven.   She asks of him :—

> " How could this Stella so confine thy will
>   To wait till she her influence distill ?"

But as he loved truly but one, that must be sufficient
apology.

The reader will now see Shakespeare's scope for satire,
and his object in feigning futilely and sinfully to claim
his friend's mistress as his own, and why he assumed her
darker and darker in act and deed.   It was Sidney's
misfortune to become infected with the Petrarchian
element, but lacking that great master's wisdom and
forbearance, he wove his thoughts into Sonnets, and rendered himself miserable and ridiculous in vainly pursuing
a futile love.   Sidney pictured Stella (the Lady Rich) for
his sister, in her early prime of beauty and virtue ;
Shakespeare pictured, for her son, the same lady late in
life, as Lady Rich and the mistress of Mountjoy.   Shakespeare takes his key note partly from a Sonnet in which
Sidney asks Stella, in allusion to her eyes, why nature
made her so black, and yet so bright ? was it to please—

> " Or would she her miraculous power show,
>   That whereas black seems beauty's contrary,
>   She even in black doth make all beauty flow ?"*

And when Shakespeare tells her to " buy terms divine," he but recals to her Sidney's words, in which she was told that she was—

> " Rich in those gifts which give the eternal crown."†

Sidney, we are told, repented of his crime ; it is to be hoped the still more unfortunate Penelope Devereux also became penitent.‡ Their love history is summed up in one line :—

> " The course of true love never did run smooth."

---

* The reason why Shakespeare speaks so vaguely of the colour of the mistress's hair, and yet mentions her eyes and brows as being black, is on account of her not being blest, as Penelope was, with that rich though rare contrast, black eyes and golden hair, or, as Sidney says—
"Rather call them her beams."
The colour of the hair of Herbert's mistress being, though dark, not absolutely black, the poet avoids alluding to it (except ironically), that his satire may be more direct in its application to the mistress of Sidney. Shakespeare also in Love's Labours Lost, spends some sparkling wit on the conceit of Sidney's mistress being beyond all others the fairest, yet the darkest, and though the brightest yet the blackest. This boast of her poet lover alas proved too true. In the comedy, the allusion to the " gracious moon " may be to Queen Elizabeth, as the "attending star " denotes Stella.

† The excuse Bryskett records Sidney made for others, should be accorded to Sidney himself :—" Let us love men for the good is in them, and not hate them for their evil."

‡ It is somewhat remarkable that the letter which Sir Fulke Greville, the friend of Sidney, wrote " to a right honorable lady" should have been permitted to have lain so long unnoticed by the critics, since it is unmistakably addressed to the Lady Rich. It was not printed till after Sir Fulke's death. The letter itself, though unfinished, occupies a large number of pages. A mere outline of it will discover to whom alone it must refer. The letter was written when she was contemplating divorce from her lord, at the time Mountjoy became her lover. The epistle is throughout a moral and religious exhortation to act true to her husband, even though he fails to merit it. She is told that to leave him, according to the laws of England, would brand her with infamy ; the only divorce she may

Q

Sidney's folly is a spot upon his sun, though only observable to discerning eyes, his Sonnets having been so seldom reprinted that few readers have met with them, and his biographers have been silent upon the subject of

virtuously look for is the divorce of death. The opening lines tell us that she had sought his advice how to act to effect a separation in the best mode :—" Right honorable Lady,—You are desirous, in regard of the trust you put in me, to understand mine opinion how you should carry yourself through that labyrinth wherein it seems time and mischance hath imprisoned you." Her excuse to Greville was the injustice of her husband —of his having a mistress, of which Lady Rich elsewhere speaks, whom, it appears from the letter, was far inferior in beauty to the wife; but Greville will not take part in her resolution. He exhorts her to bear all, live amicably with her lord, and leave the rest to heaven. He evidently viewed her at this time (and perhaps justly) as a virtuous, injured wife ; but for her fair name, and for the sake of her children, she is to bear all patiently. She will then gain her husband's love, the good opinion of the world, and " receive the immortality of good ;" but if she fails to take his counsel, she will receive universal shame, her errors will lead her to " the eternal curse of sin." He speaks emphatically of her unfortunate marriage with a rich lord, whose wealth gives him power. The description he gives of her husband is exactly the character of Lord Rich. " I know your husband's nature—rather weakly than strongly evil ; full of respects, desires, fears ; jealous and careless ; factious and unresolute ; rather inclining to craft than to violence ;—a tyrant (in words) valiant over a wife." Greville wishes her to view her misfortune as an interposition of Providence, all for the best, and in this extract appears to refer to Sidney's death, and the romantic love they bore for each other. Referring to his discourse, he calls her attention to its application :—" Now, madam, if you apply this to yourself, it hath this morality in it, to let you know that without your husband's unkind dealing, you would perchance have doted too much on the worship of one man, rejecting for that one humour all other ways of honour, as bewitched affections used to do. It seems by the providence of mischance you are driven from these narrow sanctuaries of self-affections." He apologises for his impertinent counsel, because it may lead so much to her advantage ; and though she is greatly tempted, she is to imitate Job's constancy. It appears she could not endure the grave, moral, unsympathetic tone of the letter, and acted according to her own dictates ; hence the letter was left unfinished. Greville saw the inevitable consequences arising from such a course, and deserves praise for seeking to avert them. Greville imitated Sidney in all his better parts ; he even wrote the same number of sonnets, but they neither deserve the censure due to Sir Philip's as to subject, nor the praise as to merit ; they are of an innocent

his romantic love affair ; or have but touched slightingly upon it, but the time is now come when the explanation is called for, and as his Sonnets are in part the object of Shakespeare's satire, it is given here.

---

nature, and poor in conception. Sir Fulke wrote a memoir of his friend, in which he highly extolled the "Arcadia," but says not a word of his great poetical work, "Astrophel and Stella." He undoubtedly viewed that performance as a blot upon his fame. The letter above referred to is only to be found in the edition of Sir Fulke Greville's poems printed in 1633.

FINAL REMARKS.

THE singularity of the conceit of Shakespeare claiming the mistress of his friend as his own, though she was really the friend's love alone, was a purposed imitation of the extravagant assertions and eccentric loving of the Italian and English sonnetteers. As remarked in Preliminary Observations, it was their custom to entertain a futile love. Sidney we have seen declared he was not ashamed to address Stella in bewitching sonnets as his own after she was the wife of another; hence Shakespeare's fantastic imitation with a view of satire.[*]

That it was a concerted scheme between the poet and his friend that a poetical diary should be formed of passing events connected with their mystical friendship is shown in Sonnets 34, 36, 88, 95, and 96, in which the poet reminds his friend that he is to record his faults, and in Sonnets 61 and 117 the friend is reminded that he is to record the errors of the poet. This mutual record is kept in the last twenty-eight. In Sonnets 139 and 140, the poet is to speak of the faults of the mistress, and in the 142nd she is to speak of her own, as he does

---

[*] The reader must remember that the poet does not point alone at Lady Rich, though by her being the foremost sonnetted lady of the age, and having proved, as represented, so corrupt in her wedded love to wedded lovers, the allusions are chiefly to her.

of his; and in the 151st, were she to denounce the
poets's faults, she would be but urging her own. Hence
the scheme was of mutual approval, and each understood
its significance and application. The friend of Shakespeare, like the poet, may have merely affected to be in
love with the mistress; he was probably delighted with
her for joining them in their sonnet scheme, and making
up the friendly trio. It may have been her office to
speak of the Sonnets, and circulate them so as to come
into the hands of Lady Rich, the one whom they (the
last series) were intended to represent in not very flatter-
ing pictures, reflecting, as shown, her image and acts.*
Upon the part of Herbert's lady friend, she would well
know that Shakespeare's allegorical love for her was but in
contrast to the Muse's allegorical love for the friend; for
in the address to the mistress the poet not only conceives
that she is his mistress, but that she is wedded to him in
like mystic allegory as is the friend to the Muse; and she
is also desired to view their mutual friendship, as converted, by the process of allegory, to loving wedlock,
to pursue a scheme perhaps unattainable any other
way, and in which she delighted to join, though she

---

* It is on record that Herbert, Southampton, and other lords, were frequently in the company of Lady Rich at the date 1598 to 1602, which
was just the time these Sonnets were written; they, being friends of
Mountjoy, would witness more of her mode of life than was observed by the
world, and would perhaps see the effect these Sonnets, apparently penned for
another, would have on her. This would resemble the play scene in
Hamlet. The Sonnets may have been the things to touch her conscience.
See letters of Rowland White, the post-master, to Sir Robert Sidney,
Governor of Flushing, by whom he was employed to notify to him the news
of the court.—*Collins Memorials of State,* 2 vols, folio, 1746. We have seen
Shakespeare warns his friend in Sonnet 70 to avoid mixing too much with
those whom the world censures, lest he should be slandered with them.

did not think it prudent to comply with every condition of the allegory, not even in idea alone, since the poet entreats her in vain to delude herself with the belief that the two friends are but one. Though he sometimes deludes himself that he has taught her, not in vain, to deceive herself with the same belief with which he deceives himself, that he is alone her lover, and she alone his love, yet this self delusion he discovers to be but a dream. She will not give her soul up to this belief;* but the poet resolves, upon his part, though she may still disregard his love, to blindly think she loves him and no other; and in the 151st, which is a reflex of the 136th,† he feigns to give himself entirely up to the belief that he is her real lover, and is beloved by her. The poet sportingly uses every argument to induce her to believe so; he requests her to devise any self flattery to accomplish it—to love him among a number, or to accept his love as nothing, so she loves that nothing, or to love but his name; she will then have her heart's desire, her loving William. In the 138th he pictures to her the happy result of such mutual flattery. The mere apprehension delights him; he will not only gain an attractive mistress, but in idea will be also young and beautiful. If she will fully believe this, he will consider his wish to be

---

* Shakespeare may, for the definite purpose already shown, appear to speak slightingly of the soul; yet he evidently viewed our bodies but as worthless cases containing that heavenly jewel. The 146th Sonnet, addressed to the soul, proves the poet's belief in a future reward of virtue; the 55th also attests his belief in the day of judgment; his will, in the divinity of Christ; and his dramas in the Bible as the book of God.

† In the 135th and 136th, Will is harped upon in imitation of Rich in the Sonnets of Sidney; in the 135th, line 2, he pleasantly hints that though she is not Lady Rich, she is "rich in Will."

accomplished. If demanded why this belief is entertained, an excuse is proposed: the poet may say, love being trust, he lovingly believed his mistress; and as the lover does not like to have his years told, the mistress will be silent. Thus each will lovingly deceive the other. But all without avail. Had she complied, he would have ceased blaming her; but since she would not, in pursuance of the satirical allegory, she who is the most beautiful he views as least so, on account of the sweet thief of love taking his friend from his Muse, for which reason he assumes he has a right to poetically feign he is her lover and she his love. Thus the poet alternately praises and blames her, feigns to be rejoiced and then again to be depressed. Sometimes he views her in mental vision as a bright angel, sometimes as a dark one; sometimes, in a brief interim of self delusion, he praises her, but, for reasons fully shown, she is far oftener denounced and reproached in the severest and bitterest language he could devise. In strong allegorical language he had also blamed the friend, though not to the extent he blamed the mistress. Besides, the Muse everywhere apologises or makes the most loving excuses for the friend, who is praised almost throughout the entire poem to him; and even in the section devoted to the mistress his cause is advocated. But it is not so with the mistress; she receives an equal measure of praise and blame, and finally is left, in her relation to both the poet and the friend, open to allegorical censure. Sometimes the poet offers feigned excuses for her, at other times she is told she has a right to excuse herself by saying : " I once loved you, but finding my eyes too killing for you, I turned them from you; but I am justified in doing so, it being to your other self, your friend ;"—implying that she justly regards him with loving looks only, but she really loves the friend (see Sonnet 139). She can thus give a just and loving reason, so the poet must not think himself slighted. Again, placing the picture in a different light, he tells how he madly views her, seeing her falseness, as altogether unlovely in his mind's eye, and unworthy of being loved (Sonnet 141), and all he has gained is but pain—the pain of unrequited love. So he resolves to make love to her spirit, which he had conjured up, since he cannot have the substance. In the 142nd he refused, for his Muse's sake, to give up the friend, at which denial she flies from his vision, thus implying that her spirit had pursued the poet; to discover if it was in his heart to give up the friend. At his refusal she at once leaves him, but the poet in imitation of Sidney and others, childishly pursues her love, entreating her to return to him, as he assumes that he is her real lover, both in christian name and person. But as she does not, he consoles himself with the belief that his friend will eventually return to his side, to be the comfort of his Muse (Sonnet 144); so that at times, during absence, the spirits of both the friend and the mistress visit him, and then again fly from his vision. The friend is an object of joy to his musings; the mistress necessarily one of grief. The one he fears losing, the other he despairs of gaining; and as he had concluded the counterpart series to the friend with self reflections (Sonnecs 63, 64, 65), so he appends Sonnet 144 to the series addressed to the mistress.

After an interim of some months, upon his return he praises her lips (Sonnet 145), but only for the words of pity which he feigns, she uttered when she saw his woful state, how much he must have pined for her society and love, which is but an echo of what he had told the friend (Sonnet 28) would be the case when they again met; and though the mistress pities him, she does not actually say she loves him, but he imagines her words imply as much. Having deluded himself with the feigned belief that he has won her love, and that she views him as her real lover, and as he views himself as the young and beautiful friend (see Sonnets 22, 39, 42, and 62),* and flatters himself that she believes so too, he may well consider himself as young and beautiful, and the possessor of a fair lady for his mistress. This induces him to end his complainings and pen her the love Sonnet under notice (the 145th); and to mark the change in her, and as an end to the argument, he alters its structure; and as

---

* It is worthy of remark that the poet does not, in the renewal to the friend, pen any more Sonnets bearing the mystic burthen, " My friend and I are one." The reason is explained in the counterpart renewal to the mistress. The poet may now no more merely assume so, he flatters himself that he actually is the young friend, and that he has attained the object sought for when giving this idea expression, so that in the renewal series to the friend there is no further occasion to recur to it ; but in the renewal series to the mistress the fallacy of the delusion is too evident for silence or satisfaction in the belief. It is too apparent she does not think him the young and beautiful friend, and that she has robbed both the poet and his Muse of the love first devoted to and claimed by them ; hence the allegorical jealousy and expostulation ; and because the mistress shall be defeated in the possession of the friend, in the renewal to him the poet again and again asserts or denies the wedlock of friendship, and the marriage to the Muse. Thus the poet is ever ready to bend to his friend's will, the while their mental alliance becomes faster bound, by enduring wreaths of perennial verse.

conclusion to the foregoing set penned to her, which he
purposed should be mainly satirical, he appends one
alluding indirectly, like the rest of the latter Sonnets, to
the immoral lady before referred to, who was the soul of
the age of vanity and false outward show. She is
earnestly besought to prepare for a pure eternal life :—

" Within be fed, without be Rich no more" (*Son.* 146.)

After a few months' interval he pursues the theme again,
finding he had but deceived himself in his conclusions ;
yet, in spite of this, he resolves to renew the loving war,
and assert a final claim. To effect his object, the friend is
no more mentioned—a few allusions are merely made to
him, since his purpose is not now to be his friend's
second, but actual self, that he might become in imagi-
nation the entire possessor of the fair enslaver, which is
indirectly the highest flattery he could offer to her
beauty or his friend's choice ; and though he, as heretofore,
is self deceived, yet he will feign in imitation of Sidney
and others, to have claimed the victory.

He declares he is still longing, in loving madness
(Sonnet 147), to gain her love ; and though she will not
consent, yet, against her will, she is allegorically proved
to do so ; and, as a natural conclusion to his sonnetto-
mania, and in derision of others' fantastic " Ideas," he
now declares that his reason has left him ; he is desperate,
he is past cure and care,

" And frantic mad with evermore unrest."

Personifying the mistress as Lady Rich, the poet declares to her that she had led him to believe she was
radiant and beautiful, when she (the fair woman with a

black soul) proves as dark as night and black as hell.* He
then turns off into the lachrymal strain : he blames his
eyes for viewing her as fair who is false, but excuses their
mistaking vision, they being full of tears. He thus
artfully mocks the childish sonnetteers, whose eyes were
ever showering large rain drops. He may now well ask
her whether she does not think that he loves her. He
offers her all devotion (Sonnet 149) ; he would renounce
his dearest friend if that friend did not love her ; but he
despairingly and derisively tells her to love the eyes of
another who can see she loves him (the friend) ; but he
will still delude himself, he will be blind, i. e., not observe
it. Having such influence over him, he may well ask her
how she gained such power over his heart, his eyes,
and his mind (Sonnet 150) ; how is it, when he sees
more cause to hate her, he loves her the more ? Then,
if he loves the sweet thief who has unjustly sought to
steal the friend from the poet and his Muse, she should
love him, even though he seeks to steal her from the
friend.

The excuse for such apparent want of conscience
(Sonnet 151) is that Love is too young to know what it
is ; yet all know a knowledge of right or wrong proceeds
from love, and his loving conscience tells him he may
justly claim her, so the gentle cheater is from henceforth
to accuse the poet no more of what she has supposed a
fault, lest she should turn the accusation against herself.
Each being guilty of the same fault, the poet, upon his

---

* The reader has seen she proved no true star as predicted by Sidney,
she would ever appear but an ominous flaming Comet, converting the paradise of love to its abode of torment and despair.

part, can see no reason to accuse himself, and he, having shown that he and the friend are one, may well boast of her love, and profess himself her most loving, most humble servant. Though finally accusing both himself and the mistress, and summing up their mutual faults (Sonnet 152), he declares she knows that by loving her he is forsworn, having vowed his poetical love to the friend, and by now vowing it to his friend's mistress; but she is (allegorically) twice forsworn, which makes her resemble a deceiving wife (Lady Rich). But the mistress's faults are trifling in comparison with the poet's, for he has tried to view her, as he had viewed and proved the friend with a happy result, as not allegorically vile. The mistress's actions, however, would not stand the ordeal, and the poet, in the endeavour to place her in a fair light, though using the most subtle reasons for her allegorically sensual fault, has but corrupted himself, and appears ten times more guilty than she had proved; and he in the end but personates a deluded self-deluding husband and a frantic idiotic sonnetteer.

And since he has now lost all faith in her, and his words, in seeking to vindicate her, prove so foully false, he ceases to advocate her cause, and determines to reconcile himself by the loving delusion that she is alone his mistress and he is alone her lover; hence the loving war is ended.

He concludes the Sonnets addressed to her, written in derision of the self-described lunatic lovers (the sonnet-teers), and as a covert satire on corrupt wedded love, with an allusion to the famous medicinal Bath waters, and to those who resorted to them. Harrington, in an Epigram, says they were chiefly visited by those who desired " to see and to be seen." The allegory is ended by the poet relating how he had sought to cure his mad loving fever, but without effect ; in which he resembles the poets of that day—they began in despair, and ended despairing of either ceasing loving or of gaining the object of their love. As an apology for her coldness for him, he being a rejected lover, and for the strange loving malady, with which he feigns he was possessed, he assumes that the torch of love was extinguished in the wells, now a bath, hence Cupid had not warmed her breast with love for him because a maiden of Diana's, a lover of chastity, had put out the torch of Cupid while the love God was sleeping, *i.e.*, asleep to the poet's loving interest. From love's fire the waters received perpetual heat, but at the eyes of the poet's mistress Love again lit his torch, and to try its effects, inflamed the poet's breast with love ; and though the waters put out Love's fire, they could not his—his loving desire for her could not be extinguished. Thus, the poet ends his allegory of the triumphant power of his love, showing that he is forced to love, in spite of all his Muse inspires him to say against her ; and the poet and the Muse are alike flattered that they gain the victory of love over even Love himself. He finally claims her as his own ; as in the counterpart series the friend is claimed alone for himself and his Muse. There was no remedy but for the poet to remain her devoted lover, and to believe in the sweet flattery, that she loved him and no other, just as the sonnetteers and the doting " cornuted gentry " gave themselves up to a like delusion.

It is true Shakespeare could have effected this object in a

drama, but certainly not so effectually as in the same species
of verse, which it was his object to parody. Cervantes, when
he desired to ridicule the romancists, wrote a romance.
Each aaccomplished the task they set themselves in their
own method. The fashionable absurdity Sonnetteering
had become, like the tales of knight-errants, extremely
ridiculous—both are now of the past. Shakespeare and
Cervantes brought them to the crowning-point of ridicule.
All the great dramatists of Shakespeare's day have spoken
contemptuously of Sonnets. It is then no wonder that
their chief should take the lead in bringing them into
complete derision, in an allegory, written, perhaps, in imitation of Spenser's "dark conceit." Probably Shakespeare intended the Sonnets to remain a mystery, since
he has enshrouded every clue to their unravelling with
a veil. He appears to deny the Marriage to the
Muse ; in the poem to the friend he uses every artifice
throughout many of the Sonnets to conceal the sex
addressed. It is also equally perplexing (without the
key) to discover who is the speaker, whether it is the
poet or his Muse, or both in one person, and the
person addressed, whether a male or a female, or both, as
the poet assumes actually was the case. The difficulty is
as great in the poems to the mistress, to find whether she
really was the mistress of the poet or of the friend, or
whether each could with equal right claim her. The
key, which the reader possesses, fitting all the wards of
this most cunningly devised and most intricate lock, we
believe to be the one long lost, and formerly in the possession of the " private friends " only. Shakespeare himself would give no explanation more than the Sonnets

contained; nor would he make further excuse, as the poems themselves contain every apology: they praise marriage; they uphold virtue, and denounce vice; they extol pure friendship, and censure corrupt wedlock. What apology was needed for poems bearing such arguments? It is evident it was not the intention of the poet to explain the mystery, nor would it have been wise for him to have pointed out the poets, the great persons, and their illicit loves, whom he, so subtly and fearlessly satirises; he preferred letting the Sonnets take their course, for or against him. Possibly, had he lived longer he might have given the solution of the Sonnets, and explained to whom they referred. It probably never occurred to Shakespeare that the incredible depravity some have wrongly imputed to ancient poets, would also be imputed to him. He evidently, justly viewed in the right light the love evinced by philosphers, poets, and others of antiquity for noble youths, and the love of discreet matrons for maidens, as friendships of most virtuous purity—as affections becoming the dignity and years of maturity; and like them looked on the season of youth as the fittest time to set the seeds of wisdom and example, "Honi soit qui mal y pense." Prynne, who would have said the worst of Shakespeare, is silent in dispraise of his moral character.

I have not discovered whether any writer anterior to Shakespeare treated his Muse as a real person; but I find a few years later, in 1634. that an anonymous writer, probably a dramatic poet, published an ingenious poem, which he styled "Pasquils Palinodos," in which the Muse is so much a real person that the poet describes her as

madly running away from him, through Temple Bar, along
the Strand to Westminster. He entreats her to return,
but to no purpose. She is very severe in censuring the
times, and the poet warns the good, easy cuckolds to keep
in-doors, lest his Muse should spy out their horns. She
becomes nearly mad, and the poet has great difficulty in
restraining her; to bring her to a pleasant humour, he
resorts to a tavern, and, says the poet, "My Muse and I"
fell to drinking sherry and sack. She soon becomes
merry, and sings a long, witty, and most pleasant song on
the efficacy of sack.

That Shakespeare dearly loved his friend is evident,
and that he loved him for his beauty, wit, and accomplishments is also clear, but that for which he loved him most
was the proffer of friendship he made, unsought for,
unlooked for.* The poet probably never loved any other
friend so much; at least, he has left no testimony of
such an affection, though he certainly received at one
time the patronage of the Earl of Southampton, but
there is no proof that that existed more than a few
years. Shakespeare's lofty intellect was pre-eminently
formed for a male friendship; not that he was a myso-
gynist, or that while penning the Sonnets he disliked
the virtuous of the sex; these very Sonnets prove that
he loved them, but, as observed, it was not the purpose
of his allegory to praise them. The full witness of his
love for them he has left in his dramas, wherein he
expresses his true sentiments in regard to them.

---

* Lord Pembroke's epistles to his friends, evince great love and a strong
zeal for friendship, unusual even for those times, when friendship was
justly looked upon as the foremost attribute of a gentleman.

And here it may be as well to observe the great mistake many commit in viewing these Sonnets as a literal record, made by the poet for self-condemnation, as if the poet, extolled by his contemporaries for his shrewdness and wisdom, would have had the incredible folly to have exposed a sinful life, and design that work to remain a perpetual and glorious monument. We hope from this time to hear no more such malicious charges made against our great, wise, and highly moral poet. If Shakespeare was a slave to anything, it was to his profession and interests, and not to such a love as he pictures here. When he speaks of a deep grief for the loss of his son (Sonnet 37), or for the loss of early friends (Sonnets 30, 31), he is speaking of real sorrows ; but the feigned heart-wound, for the assumed loss of the mistress, is at once evident as but feigning the loss is merely in idea, like the assumed loss of the friend. And can there be greater proof that the whole is but allegorical than the language used toward the friend, merely for giving countenance to and accepting the offerings of another Muse, and in Sonnet 116 it is clearly seen that it is a marriage of the mind alone. In brief, I contend that it is impossible to solve the Sonnets, if viewed as literal, either by rearranging them, or by supposing them as written to various people, or for others, as was sometimes the custom. They bear a mystic burden, in which they resemble no other Sonnets : besides which the poet repeatedly tells us they are,—to one, of one, and for one,—and that the mistress series was written at the instigation of the friend, who was " the only begetter " of them—in other words, it was at his desire the whole of them were written. We have seen the poet had three objects in view, firstly, writing allegorically of pure friendship and the Marriage of the Muse, secondly, of his friend's loving and patronage to others, thirdly, satirising mistress's sonnetting, and pointedly alluding to Lady Rich.

If it should be contended that both the friend and the mistress are but imaginary characters; it will not affect the explanation of the Sonnets as a satirical allegory; there can be but one solution of them in their order and entirety; but as to the reality of the friend and the mistress, there can be no reasonable doubt.

In his devoted friendship for a young nobleman Shakespeare resembles the great Michael Angelo, who bore unbounded love for the noble youth, Cavalieri.* Vasari says he could have obtained anything from Michael Angelo. Varchi, the professor extolled in the highest terms the young Cavalieri, in a lecture he gave at the Florentine Academy, as the most attractive young man he had ever become acquainted with. This lecture was on a sonnet by Michael Angelo to Cavalieri, which Varchi recited. It contained the highest flattery a beautiful youth could receive from intellectual age, yet who ever doubted the morality of the divine Michael Angelo; and what should we now say to an essay by Bacon on a sonnet by Shakespeare to Herbert. The lecturer's object was to incite the young Florentine students to emulate Cavalieri, so that they might like him become worthy of the friendship of such a man as Michael Angelo. The artist was delighted with his young, beautiful, and intellectual patron-friend, and besides writing sonnets to him, he

* See Herman Grimm's Life of Michael Angelo, translated by Fanny Elizabeth Bunnet, 1865.

executed for him many fine drawings and other works;
he could not have obtained a better man for his friend;
the great sculptor was at once rigidly moral, eminently
intellectual, and religious. His wonderful compeer,
Raffaelle, also wrote sonnets; but what have come down
to us are but of the ordinary amorous character: they,
however, show the hand of a master.

Herbert appears to have been the very counterpart of
Cavalieri; for nobility, beauty, refinement, and friendship. The engraved portrait of him in Walpole's Royal
and Noble Authors, fully bears out the praise given him,
by Shakespeare's Muse.*

Some have spoken of Shakespeare's Sonnets as his
greatest works. Without going to such a length, it is
true they are his masterpiece in a strictly poetical sense,
being written in alternate rhyme; others view them
in the opposite extreme, and speak of them as being
unworthy of the poet, which they would be, were they
written merely for the sake of writing sonnets; had they
but observed that Shakespeare devised to ridicule sonnetto-
mania—they would then, read our poet's work—

"In the same spirit that its author writ."

And though his Sonnets are but a species of parody, yet,
coming from the hand of such a master, they are of such
beauty and majesty, and of such lofty diction, that no other
sonnets can be in any way compared with them, unless it
be the few Milton penned with a like masterly vigour;

---

* And though this praise has received from various writers a gross interpretation, instances need not be given of pure fervent love, having been
construed into the vilest derangement of lust; the world being prone to
view in the worst light, that which they cannot comprehend.

in brief, Shakespeare's Sonnets are works of the highest art. But Shakespeare had a higher purpose than deriding sonnetting to fulfil; his destined "fine issue" was to teach philosophy, justice, morality, virtue, and religion, to thousands who would never listen to any other than the voice of an actor, for whom the poet has conceived acts and declamations that have ever, and ever will, receive rounds of applause.

Finally, the author apologises to his readers for all the wearisome repetitions and defects. The former, the nature of the work at least to some extent, rendered unavoidable; for the latter, he entreats their pardon, since the only apology he can make is, that he has sought assiduously to be of some service in the unfolding of our great Poet's Book of Mystery.

II. BROWN.

31, *Albert Street, Newington Butts.*

www.ingramcontent.com/pod-product-compliance
Lightning Source LLC
Chambersburg PA
CBHW030402270326
41926CB00009B/1226